Living Gay

Living Gay

Don Clark

CELESTIAL ARTS
Millbrae, California

Celestial Arts
231 Adrian Road
Millbrae, California 94030

First printing, July 1979

Made in the United States of America

Library of Congress Cataloging in Publication Data
Clark, Donald Henry, 1930–
  Living gay.

  1. Homosexuals. 2. Homosexuality. I. Title.
HQ76.25.C52   301.41'57   79-50859
ISBN 0-89087-189-2

1 2 3 4 5 6 7—85 84 83 82 81 80 79

Dedication

For the children, women, and men
whose footsteps made this path;
those who walk it with me;
and those whose truth will find it
when we have gone.

Contents

Introduction

My first-grade teacher wrote on my report card the words that should probably one day be on my tombstone: "Donald is very slow but very thorough."

It was the letters that finally did it. Ever since the publication of *Loving Someone Gay* I have received a constant stream of letters from readers who want to share something important with me. Sometimes they have questions, sometimes they just want to talk to a kindred spirit. The first few months after publication were disorienting, since I was trying to maintain my normal life as a clinical psychologist in private practice, a teacher, and, more important, a father and a lover, while doing publicity tours, media interviews and autograph parties. I was so distracted that I did not realize until months later how much I had learned during that period. But slowly I recognized that a common thread ran through the letters and the comments of people I was meeting. They said they appreciated learning about *me* in the book, because it was helpful to identify with my experience, thoughts, and feelings and those of my clients and friends. It took a while but I got the message. Readers wanted more and they wanted it in the form of simple truth about me and the people I know.

One day I realized that this book had been taking shape in my mind for a long time. A friend asked what the next book was going to be about and without a moment's hesitation I said "About living, loving, aging and dying as seen from a gay perspective."

I was lying in bed the following Saturday morning, allowing a luxurious half hour to wake up and musing about how the gay experience provides a unique perspective to help both gay and non-gay people find the personal meaning of their lives. I looked at a beautiful antique mirror that hangs on the wall—a gift from a friend. It is old glass and the reflections are not uniform and accurate as they are in new factory-made mirrors. The mirror is unique in its construction. Its inconsistencies are reliable in their own way, and the reflection of the world that you see when you look into the mirror depends both on the way the mirror is constructed and upon the point of view that you choose when looking. I started thinking of myself as that sort of mirror. My experiences have made me unique. Unlike the mirror on my bedroom wall, my experiences will continue to happen and will slowly change and reshape me, but at this moment I am like the mirror, reflecting back images of life dependent on my composition and the viewer's vantage point. And not only do I contain my own experiences, but those entrusted to me by clients and friends. I can share all of that in my reflections.

Of course, the word *reflection* has another meaning when you use it to speak of turning things over in you mind. The reflections I share here are the turnings of my mind, my attempts to understand things from various points of view.

In my own searching and reflecting, certain books have meant a great deal to me: Christopher Isherwood's *Christopher and His Kind*; Tennessee Williams' *Memoirs*; Kopay and Young's *The David Kopay Story*; John Rechy's *The Sexual Outlaw*; Kate Millett's *Sita*; Rita Mae Brown's *Rubyfruit Jungle*; and Arnie Kantrowitz' *Under the Rainbow* to name some. I wanted to know how those particular years in Germany and England were for Isherwood as a gay person, and how it had been for each of the others in their own times and circumstances.

As a gay person, I wanted news of my *family*, a sense of my roots, perhaps. I want to know what has been passed on to me by my gay sisters, brothers, fathers, mothers, grandfathers and grandmothers. I want to see how we have adapted and changed with the changing world. We have such a long history—as long as human history. And it was only one hundred years (from 1869 to 1969) from the time Benkert coined the word *homosexual* and joined Ulrichs in saying it was ". . . inborn and unchangeable, but not any more pathological than color blindness" to the Stonewall riots in New York City, where gay men and women announced they had endured second-class citizenship long enough. It is in that context and in the spirit of family that I now share my own life and experiences.

There are two questions repeatedly asked about *Loving Someone Gay* that I should answer here. Why had I insistently used "Gay" rather than "gay" throughout the book? Answer: Because I wanted to point out that we are a cultural subgroup rather than a state of mind, but having made my point I am now willing to use the English language in the same way other writers are using it. Why do some gay women insist on being referred to as lesbians? Answer: Because they want to make it clear that the experience of being both gay and a woman carries a double oppression and a special consciousness.

As you look into my mirror there are two kinds of images. You can see me musing over events past and present, constantly trying to improve my understanding of what they mean to me as a person—especially to me as a gay person. I hope you will also see yourself in the mirror, whether or not you are gay. Perhaps your image will be just different enough to start you thinking about who you are. As humans living at the same time in history, we have much to share.

This book is for people who love someone gay.

1

Searching

I saw some whales today as I looked out across the ocean. They moved smoothly through the water, breaching and spouting, as sure in their journey as they have always been. Their living, loving, aging and dying is an inevitable part of the flow of nature. Surely we humans are meant to move through our lives in the same harmonious way. But we have interfered with our natural flow. Our lives are too often unsatisfying, our loving sporadic and clouded in self-deception, our aging associated with diminished rather than enhanced stature, and our dying a fear-laden defeat shrouded in secrecy. To find harmony in our lives requires a lifetime of dedicated searching.

The search for meaning and understanding is often very difficult, yet it is the searching that makes us so alive. In these rapidly changing times it is necessary to learn that there is no destination, but that great personal satisfaction can be derived from having searched well throughout the lifetime journey. This is true for all people, but for gays it is a bittersweet necessity.

We gay people have the unique experience of being for-
eigners within our own culture. We have, of necessity, lived
in two worlds simultaneously most of our lives, and that has
made it possible for us to change our frame of reference and
gain perspective in ways that can be learned by non-gay people too. We can dare to reexamine beliefs and strip experience to the bare bone in search of truth. And it can be done
while enjoying romance and humor at the same time.

We humans are more alike than we are different. It is this
simple fact that makes me want to share the perspective of
the gay experience in the hope that it can help us all to find
more clues about how to stay afloat in the tide of social
change that is moving faster and faster everyday. What
worked fairly well yesterday may not work at all tomorrow.
It is difficult to maintain that core sense of self when the
world and you are changing so fast. But because we have a
lot in common as contemporary humans, it is the *differences*
in our individual experiences that can be used to teach one
another. Life seen from another point of view, the concepts of
bicultural people—these can be our springboard for new understanding.

We must learn to be more alert and to *notice* our surroundings and our feelings. When habit or custom cause us to over-
look the obvious, we often may miss the chance to evaluate
new concepts or entertain new possibilities. Some years ago,
my family and another daringly decided to visit a nudist colony.

There was much nervous joking in advance. The teenage
son of the other family declined to accompany us, no doubt
fearing embarrassing erections, but their six-year-old son
came along happily. During the drive, I remember thinking it
odd that we would go to so much trouble to see this "foreign"
world where naked people lived close to nature. Were we just
using the visit as an excuse to see one another without clothing? Surely in a sane world we could have stayed home and
done that (but this was before the days of hot tubs!).

We had not been among the nudists very long before we

observed that the "regulars" put a lot of energy into not noticing that people are naked; there was lots of eye contact and NO eye-genital contact. Odd. We were sitting in a luncheonette that looked like ordinary luncheonettes in small towns all over the nation, except that the only clothing being worn was one small apron on the woman behind the counter. The six-year-old duly commented on how funny it looked and how it made it "harder not to look at her boobs!" The naugahyde felt cool and sticky on bare, nervous bottoms.

While we were waiting for our grilled cheese sandwiches, a young man with a ponytail and a very attractive body made a casual entrance. I was sneaking appreciative glances at his naked form when my four-year-old daughter said, too loudly, "Look, Daddy, there's a woman with a penis."

I quietly told her that he was not a woman with a penis, but a man with a ponytail. She was insistent, and loud about it. She had probably always suspected such a possibility and thought our determined assertion that only males had penises the work of spoilsport parents. As she loudly proclaimed her joy at having discovered a lady with a penis, people in the luncheonette began to squirm. Then I noticed that no one was looking at us or at the young man. Worst of all, no one was laughing! When a lady with a penis is announced it seems to me natural that people show some interest, and if a mistake has been made they ought to enjoy the laugh in it. The blushing young man left the luncheonette without waiting for his order, and everyone returned to non-awareness—except for my daughter, who still had a look of awe in her eyes, and I, who was engaged in a violent struggle to suppress the giggles.

"Not noticing" can be deadening, even when you are *pretending* not to notice. When you don't notice, you don't feel—the resulting emotions do not happen. I denied myself the curiosity, admiration and lust that I might have experienced had I openly noticed the naked young man. Some of the nudist regulars did not permit themselves the outrage, confusion or embarrassment they might have felt if they had let themselves notice my daughter's proclamation. My daughter got cheated out of the fun, adventure, and admiration of a mistake that pointed up the limited ways adults view one another. (In those days, it was still almost unthinkable that a real man could let his hair grow long.) And, finally, we did not even allow the moment of fantasy: "Gee, that *could be* a lady with a penis!"

As a gay person, I have learned in the decade since then to find "not noticing" and "not feeling" both frightening. I have learned that I tuned out too many of my feelings, particularly feelings of anger and lust, for too many years, because I had been taught that they were inappropriate. It has been a hard struggle for me to get them back and feel reasonably comfortable in acknowledging them to myself and others when I am feeling them. I need to find ways to live with my anger and lust, because I learned that denying their existence limited my awareness of other feelings, and a life without feelings is not a human life.

I probably would not bother to go to a nudist colony now. I have seen lots of people undress and am not as curious about how bodies look without clothing. But if I were to go again, I would have to admit to myself and my companions that I found the young man attractive, and I would certainly have to celebrate my daughter's whimsy with some laughter. I would also tell the young man that I was sorry we embarrassed him. There are lots of feelings to be expressed in almost any situation. First they have to be recognized and then expressed. Giving life to our feelings gives life to our selves.

Gay people frequently report feeling somehow "different" early in life: "I noticed that my interests were different;" "I thought I was the only one like me on earth." These are the common phrases used to describe awakening gay identity. I personally fought the awareness hard into the fourth decade of my life, but the awareness was there when I was four years old, and that is not uncommon. It can be lonely and it can be frightening, but awareness of being different triggers the need to search. Since we are different, we cannot follow the simple map of life that has been relatively unquestioned by most of our non-gay brothers and sisters. We must search for answers to our questions of "why me" and "how" and "are there others?" We must search for alternatives to the snug lifestyles presented for our selection.

We are lonely for companions or peers who understand what happens to a person who has set forth on such a search. Notice our favorite singers, past and present. Many people have wondered why these singers attract so many gays. There is Marlene Dietrich, in sleek evening gown or man's tails and top hat, singing with arched brow "I've been in love before, it's true. Been learning to adore—just you." There was Judy Garland, looking bewildered, brave, and vulnerable, singing, "Somewhere over the rainbow, skies are blue . . . birds fly over the rainbow, why then oh why can't I?" Carol Channing flashes her best smile, looking like she is trying hard to cover her unsureness with makeup as she covers her disappointments with forced cheer and sings "A kiss on the hand may be quite continental, but diamonds are a girl's best friend. A kiss may be nice, but it won't pay the rental on your humble flat, or help you at the Automat." Barbra Streisand presents earthiness and lack of pretension, mixed with elegance and insistence that the world accept her nose just the way it is as she sings "Memories may be beautiful and yet, what's too painful to remember we simply choose to forget. So it's the laughter we will remember. . . ."

Can you see why we listen? The ups and downs of our search are being portrayed and shared with tears and laughter. We are comrades trading war stories. Some people mistake it for cynicism but it is not. We are accustomed to raw truth and our experience has helped us to see the deceptions used to hide truth. We also know romance perks up the spirit and laughter softens pain. These entertainers help us to acknowledge the shared awareness.

Messages have comforted us along the way. They are signs that other travelers had been on the same path with the same desires, hopes, dreams, and—sometimes—despair. Last sum-

mer in London I saw *Side by Side by Sondheim.* I was swept
away as lyric after lyric reminded me of times in past years
when I had heard the words and, thinking I sensed the voice
of my people, had stored the nourishment for times when I
might feel crazy and alone in my search. *West Side Story*
opened in New York at the time I was getting married.
Though a starving graduate student, I had sent for tickets in
advance, probably because I was unknowingly being nourished by the lyrics of many Broadway shows in those days. It
is difficult to be deviant, a graduate student, and maintain integrity.

I was very much in love and excited about getting married,
but I now know the tears that I shed at *West Side Story* were
not for the Puerto Rican's struggle in New York. I heard my
people and it made me reel:
"There's a time for us,
Some day a time for us. . . ."
Many of us are plagued by a neurotic desire to find the
answer, the impossible answer. The right lover who will solve
all problems is out there somewhere. Mother will change
magically from a self-centered, shallow person to a source of
love and validation. That sort of knocking of the head against
familiar stone walls is not to be confused with searching.
Searching does not fill one with that sort of expected despair
but rather with buoyancy, discovery and anticipation. It is
not that one is on the verge of finding the *answer*; the mystery
is never solved. The excitement comes from finding another
possibility, another clue that takes us one step further in clar-
ifying the mystery. Separating neurotic elements from the
search is helpful because it conserves energy used needlessly
on neurotic pathways and makes that energy available for
searching.

One of my gay friends is a very bright, creative woman in
the middle years of life. She is alert to the neurotic elements
in her personality and always ready to rid herself of them
with great good humor. Several years ago my friend began to
join her life with that of another woman. They developed a

wonderfully unique relationship that was designed to suit the needs of two quite individual people. But there has always been a gnawing discontent by my friend. She would look for this or that flaw in her partner but, because she is bright and honest, she would admit that the "flaws" were inconsequential.

We were talking recently about how people now in their thirties had their image of the perfect mate shaped by TV and films of the nineteen fifties, and people in their forties were shaped by the romantic movies of the nineteen forties, when man mastered woman, love conquered all, and romance reigned. She had an insight while we were chatting and, speaking of her lover, said "My God, do you suppose I'm picking at her because she's not a *man* like those damned movies taught me to look for?" Another neurotic notion bit the dust.

A man friend also comes to mind. He too is gay and a searcher adept at spotting his kinks. He grew up believing he was a bad person and finds that the neurotic need to seek reassurance of his worth pops up now and then in his searching. He has chosen to be a teacher because he naturally shows others how to search, rather than indulging in pedantic dispensation of information, and therefore gets lots of reward and admiration from students.

We were having dinner at the home of a mutual friend a couple of weeks ago and he started telling funny stories about himself as a teacher. He told of a student whom he had been trying to help with a special project. He liked the student enormously but he sensed that all was not well. They were searching together, but it was not working. Then he realized that the student was the All-American boy prototype from whom he had never been able to get enough approval. Confusing the project was this teacher's unrecognized need to look for signs that the student liked him and thought he was a good person. Once the neurotic thread was spotted, my friend was able to concentrate fully on helping the student learn. He no longer had to waste energy wondering if this youngster would be the magical validator of his goodness.

I have a neurotic need to be reassured that I am attractive and sexually desirable. I have never been handsome by the standards we are trained to value. I was attractive during periods of my childhood and, I think, for a few years around the time I was in the Army. But a standard pretty I am not. I have had lots of experiences that assure me of my sexual desirability but, neurotically, I tend to forget them. I am too often tempted to look for a physically stunning man who will find himself irresistibly drawn to me. It is a losing game, as are all such repetitive, neurotic habits. When I catch myself at it, I can check to see whether there is anything else happening between this person and me. If so, I can concentrate on that, and, if not, I can excuse myself and move on.

While searching does not have an end until we reach the end of life, there are resting places, discoveries, and acquisitions along the way. One of the difficult learnings is to let ourselves have what we find or earn. Perhaps this is nowhere more true than in gay pairing. I am thinking of at least six gay couples I know well as I write this. We are all well-educated and have done a decent job of raising our consciousness about our gay identities. Yet we find ourselves having silly troubles in our relationships. Too often it has to do with sexual activities or desires of one or both partners. It is transparent that we have been trained to pay too much attention to our sexuality as homosexuals, the word assigned to gay people in this society. We have also worked harder to understand human sexuality and are more clear about realities. Yet, the tension pops up in this area too often. The reason, I suspect, is that, try as we will, we still carry around too many of the myths and stereotypes that were ground into us during all of our developing years. When threatened, it is too easy to see a lover as "one of those people," "possessed with sex," "using sex as currency," "putting sex before everything else," "unable to maintain a relationship because of promiscuity," or one who "doesn't love me because his sexual attraction to me is less than mine to him."

The other strong operating factor is homophobia. We gay

people struggle to rid ourselves of this hideous gift from our culture but some of it is always with us, as it is with non-gays. When we are settled into a relationship that meets our needs, with a partner whom we admire, respect, and love deeply, life can be too good. It is as if a secret voice inside warns that when life seems this good, something must be wrong. It is based, of course, on the often silent assumption that you, as a gay person, do not deserve a life that is good. Two women or two men do not deserve to be happy together. When tensions arise, as they must in any relationship, it is too easy to assume that the tension is there because it is not right for two men or two women to be together in so intense a relationship.

So it is difficult to let ourselves have what we have gained through our search! A network of trusted friends can be a support system. For many years we have been told we are crazy and wrong. Each of us needs some people we can trust enough to ask if we are crazy or wrong at any given moment. And such trusted friends cannot repeat the basic truths too often. We need frequent reminding that we deserve the love we have found, the job we have earned, the public respect our behavior has generated. We need to be told often that it is to be expected that we will try to sabotage our happiness when our resources are at low ebb. These are reminders of basic truth. Searchers need support. People who have opted for one of society's prepackaged lifestyles find that it comes equipped with more than enough support. It may be boring but it is safe.

Searchers by nature are in new territory every day, and it does not always feel safe and secure. One of the things we have to learn is to reach out and ask for the support, not like a needy child tugging at a busy parent, but like a deserving adult consulting a peer.

Searchers fare better if we can weed out what is neurotic or unrealistic and therefore counterproductive, because it misleads us in our search. We also must learn to *become* that for which we search. It may sound mystical but it has a core of pragmatic truth.

Let us take the example of the search for a lover. I have re-

peatedly advised people to try to become the lover for whom
they search. Put the energy into becoming that which you
would discover. As you try to do this, it takes the heat off the
people whom you encounter socially. They do not see desperation in your eyes and are able to relax and let you get to
know them. The opposite happens when people sense there is
a desperate need and they are being screened as an applicant
within the first hours of meeting. There is a temptation for
them to put on a false front or to run.

When your energy is going into becoming the lover for
whom you search, you may find that some of your expecta-
tions and desires are impossible for a human being to fulfill.
You may well discover that you are incapable of being warm
and loving all the time and it is equally unrealistic to expect
someone to be that way with you. You may discover that you
do not even want to be strong all of the time, and it is prepos-
terous to think you could love someone who could pull off
such an act.

Last but not least, you come to terms with basics about
yourself, such as your looks. You can rearrange the hair and
the body weight, but there are parts of you that will always
be just as they are. You must learn to love the you that *is* if
you are becoming the lover whom you desire. When you care
for yourself deeply you communicate that to others and become much more attractive to people. By that point you will
have done a good enough job of breaking the stranglehold of
your habitual concepts of beauty that you too can see many
more people as attractive. The selection process has become
much more rich and varied.

According to Zen, "When the student is ready, the master
will appear." When you are the lover you desire, he or she
will appear.

And this is just as true in other areas of search. Become that
for which you search. It is the process, not the product that
must be the focus. It is the journey, not the destination—
otherwise you will arrive too early, unprepared for the new
scenery and folkways, wondering where you are and how to
enjoy it.

2

Once Upon a Time

I grew up by the Atlantic Ocean, walking the New Jersey shore in the winters of my childhood, searching for some understanding of myself and the world around me. Red hands in my pockets, I watched the wintry green ocean turn to white spray as wave after wave after wave found its way to the beach. The ocean's power, its constancy, held solace for a boy who could not understand why the world was the way it was. Why wasn't there enough food? Why were people so wary of one another? Why didn't we touch? Why wasn't it all right to let someone know you felt affection for him?

This morning, following a lifelong pattern, I was driving over the mountains to the beach when a movie I once saw began to haunt me. *Elvira Madigan* was a film that revealed a special love story in a series of scenes like museum paintings, accompanied by Mozart's music. Now, as I sit high on a cliff overlooking the Pacific on this sunny autumn day, I understand that the recollection of that splendid film has brought me a message from my inner being.

In the film, two people fell into a love for one another that

15

neither had anticipated, nor would they have admitted in advance that they wanted or needed it. Neither person realized the profound consequences their love would have. They were forced to defy convention and live outside their society. They endured degradation, loss of comfort and beauty, rejection by others whom they loved and trusted, and separation from the people upon whom they had depended for validation. They hurt one another and faced bleak despair. But it was never possible to turn back. Having once seen the truth of their love for one another, they knew it was necessary to follow it—as necessary as anything in human experience. In the end they chose to die, a decision as courageous, right and necessary in their circumstances as their life together had been. They had submitted to the truth of their destiny, gained what was theirs together, but lost all that each valued before they met.

Elvira Madigan was a sleeper for me. I saw it with my wife in a suburban shopping center in Westchester County, New York. Two much-loved but tiring babies were at home with a sitter; it was a good evening out for us. When the film ended, my wife and I marveled together at the visual beauty of the film—those rich paintings flowing in sequence with the music. I knew that I had been profoundly touched and disturbed, but it was difficult for me to know how.

Now I know that what the film had evoked in me was fright. I was happy. I was married to a woman with whom I could share love easily. We could be daring and iconoclastic together. We could share interests in people, music, opera, books and social causes. We valued a strong home and family life. We could appreciate one another's spontaneity. We could be unashamed in our caring for one another and voice our complaints, hurts, or annoyance when there was a need. We were popular as a couple and had wonderful friends, old and new, with whom we shared various aspects of our life. But that film touched a cnord of fear. Somewhere deep within me, I knew that could happen to me. Somehow I knew that the real me needed to share life and love with another man, that there was an empty place inside my overtly satisfied self that was aching to encounter the right man, and that if he ever appeared, all that I held dear in the present would be lost.

I wonder why so many gay people find themselves in this kind of near-perfect heterosexual marriage. I know it happens to a great number of gay men; many are friends or have been clients. I have heard similar stories from gay women who are, or were, in heterosexual marriages. Among the gay men I know best who have been in an apparently ideal heterosexual marriage, there are certain similarities. Most of them find the myth of masculinity with its code of nonfeelings and success-oriented dominance to be unacceptable. They know they are "different," and so develop a sensitivity and concern for their mate that is wide in latitude and deeply committed. There is always the risk, perhaps almost entirely hidden from self-awareness, that an irresistible same-gender mate might come along. Realization of the preciousness of the marriage and family seems heightened by the threat that it could be lost if gay feelings are revealed. No wonder friends and neighbors are shocked when such a "good" marriage ends.

I wonder if such a marriage is to be mourned, or celebrated, or both. I suppose the average person would say it should be avoided, but who knows? Among the thoroughly heterosexual marriages I have known well over the years, I can find only two that seem as rich and satisfying as were mine and those of several gay friends. Gay formerly-marrieds often ask themselves whether they should have done it. Would I do it again if I had it to do over? I know that my wife felt hurt and betrayed when we separated, yet she seems stronger and more self-sufficient today. I remember Morales, standing on the stage in *A Chorus Line*, singing "Look, my eyes are dry. The gift was ours to borrow . . . we did what we had to do . . . can't regret what I did for love." In many ways I do not regret denying my fullness of self so that I could live in the love and adventure of that heterosexual marriage. I also know that I did what I had to do when the marriage was ending for me. My eyes are not always dry, but perhaps one day I will stop shedding tears over this passage from one stage of my life to the next.

In more than a few of the letters I have received there has been the frightened, angry voice of a wife or a fiancée whose male lover has discovered and/or disclosed his gay identity (and one man came to talk to me when his wife ended the marriage and went to live with a woman lover). I read the letters and wonder what words of counsel or comfort there are. Maybe it will work out? Hang in there, help with one another's pain, try to share this even if it is the final sharing? Be good to one another? I am reluctant to say "Kiss one another one last time and say goodbye to what has been," though I am coming to believe this may be the most honest thing to do. It is so easy to sour what once was sweet. As a professional I can help a woman and man to hear one another through this agonizing period. But perhaps it is best not to stay after the party is over—just kiss and cry and say farewell, wishing each other new tomorrows that are as good as the yesterdays.

The rules of society do not help. There is too much blind insistence on keeping a couple in a marriage. Our frontier society—traditional, materialistic, religious—needed clear property rules (even when the property was another human) to maintain stability. We should be able to find social patterns that transcend that sort of anti-human mentality today. Individuals change in their long lifetimes and we could make it more graceful for them to leave that which has been outgrown. We could have fewer sour couples (portrayed on television as normal) and more alive, searching individuals in our society.

There *are* some mixed pairs, one partner gay and one not, who make marriage work for them in a manner that is fully satisfying. It seems to be easier if both the man and woman are gay—otherwise it is too hard to fully comprehend the needs and world view of the other person. I know that I tried hard to have it come out well, and I believe that the woman who was my wife tried hard to make it come out well, but we are not together now.

Often, in considering this sort of troubled situation, the gay person gets short shrift. It is as if he or she has willfully chosen to step outside the rules of society. The intimates on the sidelines often speak of the non-gay partner as being "spunky," "a very unusual person," "a remarkable woman/man." There is a quiet implication that this innocent person is saintly in her or his willingness to put up with so much from a renegade mate. Admiration runs high even if the intimates on the sidelines are gay. I believe that admiration may be justified, but the virtues of the gay person tend to be overlooked or taken for granted as *payment for deviance.*

This gay person usually has done everything he or she knows to make life fit individual truth while staying within the bounds of society. He or she has probably carried an enormous burden of guilt and becuase of it may have overcompensated in giving to the non-gay spouse. You may be looking at a strained and exhausted person who needs as much support in taking the next steps as does the non-gay spouse.

This is a good example of how a gay perspective can illuminate the experiences of a non-gay person. A non-gay woman friend said, "I think an important factor here is that greater sympathy goes to the person who is passive in the decision to split. My friends sympathized with my husband because I had *chosen* to leave. He had no choice left." She, like a gay person, is an individual who tried but could never comfortably fit any of the culturally approved roles of married woman-wife-mother. She is a person whose eyes are open to her own truth and who must forge ahead on her individual path or lose integrity and, therefore, the reason for living. She tried to make marriage fit. She, too, has been punished by family friends for her deviance. She, too, has trouble at times realizing that she is a brave and virtuous person who deserves praise and support.

The whole situation troubles me. I wish there were standard wisdom to offer both parties. I suspect that some of the sacred old notions about marriage are getting in my way: "Until death do us part," and so forth. Maybe it is not a good idea to start with the assumption that you should try to keep a marriage together if possible, using emotional bandaids, patches, or renovation. Since individuals do continually change in their needs, desires, aspirations and abilities, maybe a serious stress point in the relationship should be faced with the basic assumption that the marriage is no longer meeting the needs of the two people. From that assumption, one could begin to prepare for separation. You could still take a look at what each person is getting and *not* getting from the relationship and perhaps boldly state the changes that each would require of the other if the relationship were ever to resume.

So if we change the basic assumption from "this marriage should be saved if possible" to "this marriage should end now and start again only when and if both need and want it," we would learn to live with the pain of loss and disruption somehow—probably with much more grace. Eventually, we might expect such pain as one of the natural human emotions and not be so cowed by fear of it that we store resentments and transmute yesterday's love into thinly veiled endurance.

Perhaps the woman who learns her husband is gay (or the man who learns his wife is) could try immediately dealing with the fact that the old marriage is dead. There may still be love on both sides, but the possibility of getting married to one another again must be questioned and all factors weighed just as before the first marriage. All of this may or may not help, depending upon how thoroughly our society has trained each person to fear being or living alone. Sometimes that fear is so strong that a person will suffer almost anything to avoid being unpaired.

Looking back, I see that my marriage began slowly to pale for me a couple of years after I "came out." At least five years before we separated my wife seemed vaguely unhappy and I knew dimly that my accelerating change was making marriage feel less comfortable for me. But we attributed her unhappiness to having been transplanted from New York to California. That was safe because time and some effort could surely cure the problem. We dealt with the shadowy discomfort in many ways, including joking fantasies about how it would improve the quality of both of our lives if we brought another husband into the family, a husband for both of us. (The several couples I know who have actually tried that experiment are all now unmarried, by the way.)

During those final years there were still plenty of good times, lots of laughs, and lots of love offered and accepted by both of us. But I knew (without ever quite admitting it to myself because it was unacceptable) the total love that once existed was slipping away. I was "out" and knew I was gay. I needed to share love and life with a man. It had to come sooner or later and it came, I believe, when I was ready. I had become enough like the man I needed that we could recognize one another.

However, I hoped—against my real hope—when I first met him that it was only an infatuation which would cool. I know he hoped the same, with the same ambivalence. My guess is that both wives also hoped it was an infatuation. But the feelings kept growing in variety and depth. It was clearly love. I recognized the symptoms. He and I went away together for a few weekends, telling our respective wives where we were going and with whom, dutifully checking in by phone during the weekend, trying to retain self-respecting roles as decent, caring husbands. We told ourselves and each other that we wanted to keep our marriages and families intact. But the feeling of love inside me was growing.

One weekend in Laguna Beach he and I were sitting on a deck facing the ocean, each of us reading a book and sipping a glass of wine. The sun was lowering to the distant horizon and the air was full of peace. I felt a lump in my throat and knew I was about to cry. Confused, I excused myself to walk on the beach. He asked if I were all right and I nodded, not knowing the truth myself. Life was suddenly so rich and I was about to cry. That was all I knew. The realization had begun: It could be this easy and this good. The place inside me that had been empty for a lifetime was full. I had experienced the fitting with another man, and I knew I could never again deny my need for this totally fulfilling love.

Mixed with my joy was terror, guilt and remorse. I knew my wife deserved the same love and it was not in me. Maybe it never had been. When I talked it out weeks later with a gay woman friend, she said it all made sense, but it also made her sad because she knew and cared for my wife. I begged for advice, daring to say the word *divorce* aloud for the first time. She slid her glasses down her nose, the better to see me directly, and said, "Oh, I see! You thought you could get out of this with no guilt. I don't think you can." I have repeated her sage words to a number of people since then. Guilt is neither more nor less attractive and important than any other human emotion. It has its place in the whole array of one's emotional life. It is the reminder to think hard and check one's personal morality balance. It is important not to run from it, and it is important not to wallow in it. Let it do its job and move along like any other emotion.

In the months that followed Laguna Beach, my wife and I talked, cried, wrote notes and letters to one another and tried to make things better. We were able to make things better sometimes, but again and again I could feel it slipping away. Finally, I wrote it in a last note, saying the terrible truth as I knew it, that I needed separation and divorce. It was not so that I could run into the arms of this man, but because I was now living a lie. I knew that full love for me could only be achieved with a man, and even though she and I had shared a wonderful marriage for most of our eighteen years, and even though things were better for us than for most people right up to the end, I had to get out. I had discovered that I could love fully only with a man. Ninety percent is better than most people hope for, but it is dishonest to live that 90 percent once you have experienced 100 percent.

The months that followed were hideous. She and I were careful and honest with the children, but struck out at one another verbally in ways we had never done before. Since then things have gotten better and there are friendly exchanges at times; I still have hope that we will be real friends one day. We were, after all, friends before and during marriage.

Recently there was a flare-up of the hurt and anger again. Maybe that is how it works. Like a spiral sort of cycle or like mourning, the hurt comes less often with less intensity as time passes. This most recent flare-up happened because my lover and I finally decided we would move into a house together. The logistics of having our children live with us half time while the homes of their mothers are fifty miles apart make it necessary for us to move to the city, almost halfway between our respective suburbs. I had unwisely talked it over with the children to feel out their reactions before talking about it with their mother. Her anger focused on moving the children to the city half time; mine focused on her seeming to tell me I was not allowed to move.

It was after a birthday party for my son. She and I sat in Ghirardelli Square, the beautiful blue bay before us with its sailboats, islands, and backdrop of hills in clear autumn sunshine. And it all hurt again. I looked at our son who is so beautiful and free and thought "He came from our bodies and our love. We shared great beauty together and now we sit here torn, angry, disliking one another. There must be a better way." What if I had never married? What a lot would have been missed—the good parts that include two wonderful children and the terrible parts that include the denial of my full self for so many years and now the feeling of being tied to an old love that has degenerated so much that the friendship at its core is hard to find.

But it is silly speculation. What is *is*, and what was, *was*. This flare-up of hurt and anger is because the other shoe is dropping for both of us. Moving in with my lover is the gay equivalent of marriage. The heterosexual marriage is now clearly finished and we need to mourn it. I hurt, and I hurt for her. How will I handle it if my lover moves on? I guess I will hurt a lot and maybe I will strike out in unloving ways. Maybe. But of course, the world and I are changing every day, so I might feel less terror then. I have learned already that willingness to accept the natural flow of life, daring to change, is what permits life to be.

But I sometimes feel that I will never be free of guilt and hurt. I am sorry I did not tell her directly about the move before she heard it from the children. I am sorry I put the children in the nasty position of messengers carrying bad news. I am sorry our contract for a "forever" marriage did not fit for me for life. I am sorry, sorry, sorry. I wonder if she is sorry, or if anyone is sorry, that it took me forty-five years to discover that my life is my own, that being gay is wonderful, and that I am responsible for living my life truthfully as an adult.

Once upon a time there was a wonderful marriage. It nourished me and I grew up in it. It is finished now. I hope it did some good in her life, too, and that she can use it to move on. I guess that stories that begin with "once upon a time" do not always end with "and they all lived happily ever after." But, who does live happily ever after? If we are lucky we can say that life has been satisfying, with good times and bad, joy along with the sorrow.

I remember another film, *The Way We Were*, the Barbra Streisand/Robert Redford portrait of a marriage that went through World War II and the McCarthy era. It had lots of Southern California beach scenes and triggered many memories of my own marriage. The film showed how a once-upon-a-time marriage was good to grow up in and how it helped each of them become more of what each had always been, stronger. I think they saw that, and there was caring in their eyes when they met the last time after years of not seeing one another. There was some awkwardness in their meeting too—near strangers who had once been so intimate and shared so much—but I think there was a silent "thanks."

We must continue to question the rights and wrongs taught

us in fairy tales and myths. We must question all convention, not just marriage. Individuals continue to grow or they wither. Changes come. We continuously grow, and come out of one shell after another like a baby chick starting again and again, larger and stronger each time. But each time we step from the shell there is a period of heightened vulnerability. It is part of the growth cycle. Mistakes and regrets are to be expected, but they still hurt.

All we can do is try to get life *more* right each time we shift and change. And we can remember to thank the important people who have nourished and prodded our growth along the way. I hope to be able to exchange "thank yous" one day with the woman with whom I once intimately shared life, but it must be without the inhibition of wariness rooted in guilt and hurt.

3

Ceremony and Celebration

Two men who met in one of my groups became lovers and moved in together. One had earlier been married to a woman but had been living as a single gay man for some years. The other was still married to a woman, though near the end of the marriage, when he met his lover. Soon after they moved in together one of them discovered that he had cancer. Within a week there came the trauma of surgery and the awareness of life hanging in the balance. When he recovered from the initial surgery, the two of them decided to go ahead with a housewarming and Joining Ceremony that they had planned earlier, and asked me if I would say a few words to them and their guests.

I do not know when I have been so honored or felt so fearful that I might not be up to the task. It made me aware once more how much we gay people need ceremony and celebration. We have birthdays, like everyone, but almost every other ceremony or celebration is different for us than it is for the general population. Many are family holidays and we are not quite included in the family, or our lovers are excluded, because our status is not sanctioned by the larger community. We are like immigrants in our own nations, cut off in part from genuine participation in recognized celebrations, searching for community validation and recognition within our subculture.

A weekend out of town was cut short to get back for the Joining on a Sunday afternoon. On the plane I worried aloud about it with my lover. My own heterosexual marriage ceremony had meant a lot to me, and I knew these two men had already been through similarly meaningful wedding ceremonies of their own. How could I help to make this suitably different and yet keep the feeling of an important moment, recognized by the community, celebrating a special love and affirming their right to count on community support through difficult times in the future? And there was the cancer sharpening everyone's awareness of the importance of *now* in this relationship.

In the end, the two of them stood with me facing the guests, who watched us with shining faces. I had asked each of them to select a flower from their garden to give the other, and for the two of them to select one together that would be a symbolic gift to me and their other guests. I said a few words about the gift of love, its beauty and fragility represented by the flowers they exchanged. And I accepted the gift of their jointly chosen flower as a symbol of the way their love spread to the rest of us who cared for them, touching us with its beauty, enriching our lives, and making us more capable of showing love for them. I passed the flower they had given me to my lover who in turn passed it to the person next to him, until it had touched each person in the room. Then we took a few moments for silent celebration, they kissed, we three hugged, and then the hug spread through the room. There were tears and laugher, flashbulbs, glasses clinking together and the aroma of festive food brought by the guests. Somehow we had done it. We had recognized this union. I could feel the satisfaction in the room. Most of us were gay. All of us knew how much the ceremony was needed. My lover cried most of the way home in recognition of how sweet and how capriciously unfair life can be. Thanks to whatever gods may be, most gay people have learned how to cry and laugh, or I sometimes think we would die from too much awareness.

Every culture and subculture makes good use of ceremonies and celebrations as a stabilizing force in the society. On a day in November 1978 the San Francisco community created a new and desperately needed ceremony within a matter of hours which involved many thousands of people. On that day both the Mayor and the city's first openly gay Supervisor were murdered in City Hall. Harvey Milk was more than a gay person elected to public office; he had become a symbol of the political voice and power of the gay people of San Francisco. And the Mayor had been our friend. The gay community reacted with agony and horror. There was legitimate fear that the fuse of impotent rage would be torched and violence might take over the streets of our beloved city.

But by sundown that day word had spread throughout the gay community that we would assemble in the gay ghetto and march down the main avenue of the city in memorial procession, gathering at City Hall with our flowers and candles to share our loss together. Perhaps our quickly invented ceremony grew out of an earlier occasion when we had gathered at this same place to mourn a city employee, a gardener, who was murdered because he was gay. Whatever the antecedents of the miracle, we avoided the violence that could have erupted so easily, and honored our dead and our loss with dignity that impressed the world.

Never in my life have I felt more pride of community than when I walked down the hill from my home with my lover, arm in arm, carrying our flowers and candles, and saw dozens and then thousands of our people gathering in solemn grief, determined to honor our dead with a quiet statement of strength and solidarity. As we marched down the main avenue of the city, a sea of tiny candles burned as far as the eye could see. There were tears, muffled conversations of condolence, arms around one another. Some people were wearing *yarmulkes* and blowing the *shofar*; a black man walked alone on the sidewalk with his eyes closed singing sad New Orleans blues; some professional musicians assembled together outside of the Opera House played "Blowing in the Wind"; and Joan Baez sang as we walked the final block to City Hall. The Acting Mayor was there, the Chief of Police was there, respected leaders of our gay community were there—and we all reached out to one another with promises that we must not let this happen again, that love must be shown to be stronger than hate, and we sang "We Shall Overcome" with all of our hearts. I was so touched, and I still am, that we could create that ceremony to help heal the many thousands physically present and the hundreds of thousands who watched it on television and saw pictures of it in magazines and newspapers. We needed the ceremony and we created it in a matter of hours.

There are other ceremonies and celebrations that recognize the stages of human life and the cycles of life on our planet which we see as the changing seasons. Each ceremonial celebration calls for public attention, a recognition of the importance of the personal and community occasion. Many of the holidays also permit an outpouring of emotions that may otherwise be held in check, and thus bring increased emotional health.

One of the ceremonies we gay people need is something like a Confirmation or Bar Mitzvah—a recognition of having accepted the responsibilities and privileges of gay identity. What we call it is not so important, I guess. It could be a Recognition Day or a Coming Out Party. It requires the presence of the elders of the tribe or the pillars of the subculture and it needs the fun of congratulatory celebration. Maybe it also needs recognition gifts. Perhaps we could lead other subcultures away from the gross materialism that has lessened the human value of many ceremonies. Perhaps our gifts could be something created by each of us or something that has been held dear to each of us and helped us live better as a gay adult.

We also need something comparable to the announcement of an engagement. (There is nothing wrong with the word *engagement* except that it has become a hollow concept with little impact in the heterosexual community.) Two women sent me an invitation which read "We're Gonna Give It a Try Party. You're invited to try to be there. Try—you'll like!" This announces a relationship that is to be taken seriously, and that the two people are exploring the feasibility of making a more serious commitment to one another. It could be a party hosted by close friends with some sort of group gift to the couple, perhaps a weekend of carefree seclusion. Some could help pay for the trip and some take over responsibilities.

Joining Ceremonies already seem to be taking their place in the gay world. Usually the couple taking this solemn step (similar to marriage in the heterosexual world) creates a unique ceremony that speaks to their world of loving friends and supporters about the ways they hope their love will function. Ceremonies written by the couple happen in the heterosexual world too, but they are rare. It is an ironic gift to us that, since the standard marriage ceremonies are so infrequently made available by church and state, we must create our own, and in the creation we must search for a statement about what we mean this relationship to be. Few gay couples promise love for life, though they may proclaim their wish that it would be so. Still fewer promise obedience or monogamy—we have had to face the reality that these are difficult and sometimes damaging promises to make. Instead, the Joining Ceremony usually promises little but states clearly the hopes for the future and appreciations of the present.

Of course, we must continue to insist on the same civil rights, including legal marriage, available to other citizens. Whether or not we choose to marry in traditional ways, we will not be full citizens until we have all the rights of full citizens.

Increasingly, *house*warming is apt to mean *home*warming. Whatever the history of the two or three or four gay people creating a home together, they are now announcing that this is more than sharing the rent. They have created a home and have asked people important in their lives to enter and bless it. This sort of homewarming ceremony sometimes takes the place of a Joining. It is less likely to be solemn and more likely to be festive unless there is a staged ceremony in the midst of the party. It reminds me how diverse are the symbols we are choosing. One foursome had a housewarming and made their symbolic announcement, not with wedding rings or a ceremony, but by wearing identical outfits.

Some people are allergic to anniversaries of any sort and I can see why. I can still remember as a child seeing the picture of my grandmother and grandfather in the local newspaper, staring out at the world, announcing they had lived together for fifty years. Even at the time it struck me that it was something like announcing that they had won an endurance contest. I think anniversary celebrations are nice if they truly celebrate the joy of having shared something for another year, but too often they look like a public announcement that the couple has gotten through another year and need congratulations to bolster their strength to get through the next.

Our culture as a whole could make use of a Life Change celebration of some sort. People are living longer. More and more of them make serious changes of direction once or twice during that long lifetime. I do not know why we find it so surprising. It was not long ago in the history of human beings that people were living to the ripe old age of forty. With most people now looking at the possibility of twice that life expectancy, which is really three times as long on earth as an adult, it is no wonder some serious changes are called for periodically.

If we assume that it is healthy and necessary for individuals continually to change and grow, some major shifts become understandable. Occupations pale and new ones are sought. Marriages will wear out because two forty-year-olds are not bonded in the same way the two nineteen-year-olds were who pledged undying love. Lifestyles are reevaluated, and the corporation executive who climbed the ladder of success with little time to consider where he was going may want to sell his stock and live by a lake in Mexico, learning to grow vegetables and weaving tapestries.

A Life Change celebration would be an announcement of an individual's altered direction. It would provide comforting community support—so the person need not feel as if she or he were breaking a tribal taboo and therefore deserving of guilt. The ceremony also might cause some of the celebrants to reevaluate current status, values, and life satisfaction. With more Life Change celebrations, we might need fewer counselors or psychotherapists.

Funerals and memorial services are certainly established ceremonies in our culture, but I think we gay people must find slightly different ways of handling the profound occasion of death. Too often we have struggled for a lifetime to make a viable lifestyle that permits us to be gay and still live in a non-gay world and then, at the moment of death, non-gay biological family members take over the ceremony and exclude those people who have been most important in our life, thereby denying them public recognition of their grief and public opportunity to mourn. This also denies the deceased person's lifetime any reality.

We need funeral or memorial services that recognize gay family and what it has meant to live as a gay person. There should be recognition that it was not easy. Special congratulations are in order for a self-respecting, productive life. When a non-gay person has lived a life against greater-than-usual odds it is recognized. We deserve the same recognition.

We need to have skillful gay-oriented attorneys do some work for us while we are alive to insure that gay loved ones will not be cut out of property rights or the general rights that would be granted next-of-kin in this society. Paul Hubble, a San Francisco attorney, uses the device of appointment of conservatorship to help protect these rights while one is alive (appointing a lover or friend to next-of-kin status in making decisions if one is incapacitated and unable to do so). A careful will drawn by a gay-oriented attorney can help prevent a gay person's life from being turned into a travesty at death. If the chief mourner at a funeral is of the same gender as the deceased and it is a cause of discomfort or embarrassment to the biological family members, family friends, clergy, or the mortician, let these people stay away and let us gay people bury our dead in dignity. (If that sounds angry, it is, because I have heard too many stories about lovers waiting outside closed hospital doors and being asked not to cause a scene at the rear of a funeral assemblage.)

The sort of ceremonies and celebrations I have been musing on so far have to do with individual life passages or developmental stages. The need is just as strong for us to have our community holidays. We have started in that direction already. Our summer holiday is the annual Gay Pride Day, celebrated with parades across the nation. It comes at the end of June because it commemorates the anniversary of the Stonewall riots in New York City in 1969. Odd that it turned out to be our summer holiday, coming so near the All-American Fourth of July celebration of the ideal of independence. The parades and parties get bigger every year.

Our autumn holiday, of course, is Halloween. How it got to be a special holiday for us, I suppose we will never know for sure. A part of it is due to those brave drag queens and bull dykes of past decades who relentlessly forced the general public to face the gender caricatures which arose when people were forced to choose to be feminine *or* masculine. Cross-gender dressing became a part of our heritage. It is still frightening to many gay people who remember non-gays laughing and pointing fingers in their (invisible) presence and who vowed never to cross the proscribed gender line and be like *them.* Twisted as the roots are, it is a part of our cultural heritage and Halloween is the time of year when one has always legally been able to go out in public in cross-gender dress. We have done a lot of that, taking it a step further to

explore various parts of our identities or to display our fantasies in public. It is a be-yourself holiday, letting it all out, a
Dionysian festival like Mardi Gras. Sometimes it is a display
of questionable taste, but it does help to stretch our tolerance
for freedom of expression that does not harm anyone.

Just last year, it struck me that Thanksgiving is a family
holiday and it is a time when I could be with my *gay* family.
There are a handful of gay people to whom I feel especially
close—they are family more truly than most biological families. We stand ready to help one another through adversity
and to celebrate one another's good fortune. So my lover and
I gathered together a cozy group of these family members for
Thanksgiving and we cooked and feasted and loved together.
When we issued the invitations, several people said they
wondered why they had not thought to do it in years past.
They were more than weary of going to Aunt Matilda's or to
Mom and Dad's to hear the yearly questions from the
gathered clan about when they planned to marry and settle
down. Always before it seemed a silly holiday to me—
spending the day eating too much with relatives one did not
care about—but now I see that it can be a wonderful holiday.
We did overeat, but because it was delicious and joyful—for
the fun of it, not the duty of it, we had a wonderful sharing.

It is no news that Christmas and New Year's have become
wearisome holidays that the average citizen is as apt to antic-
ipate with dread as with joy. Christmas has become the festival of reducing retail inventory while New Year's has become the holiday of guilty partygoers wondering why they
are cursed with an inability to get into the "proper" celebratory spirit and/or how they are to deal with a hangover on the
first day of the new year.

Those of us who are gay and have children are still tied
(even if unwillingly) to the standard commercial Christmas,
since our children are prepared for it by television, school,
and sentimental stories about a world that may never have
existed. I did experience that sense of wonder and the joy of
giving as a child. One Christmas when there was no money

for a tree or presents, the tree did miraculously appear while I was asleep and we gave one another presents of things we already had. I remember my sister gave me her violin! And I remember years of careful shopping in the five-and-ten with the hoarded supply of coins hard-earned over a period of months, trying to find a special thing that would bring joy to each person on my Christmas list. But those years seem lost now in the prepackaged commercial Christmas that starts in November.

Maybe we gay people could change the holiday and put it back on the track. Maybe we could put caring back into Christmas. Maybe Christmas and Chanukah could again be holidays of shared closeness when love is freely expressed, not just with store-bought gifts, but with the labor of love. We could gather together and do things for one another or offer gifts that have been created from love. The gift could be a home-baked pie or a poem, or some needed mending. The sharing can be of hopes and dreams said quietly before the fireplace or around the table. The joy can be found in the love for one another within the assembled group which can fill the air and raise the roof.

And New Year's Eve need not be a desperate party. It could be spent alone, with one or two other people or in a small gay family group with a quiet discussion of what went right and wrong in the year before and how the next year can be better. New Year's Day need not start with a hangover but can follow a sound night's sleep on a clear conscience, filled with awareness of gay loved ones, open and alive with the fresh start of a new year.

But the holiday I most want to try to get established for myself and my gay loved ones, is a holiday that parallels the Seder celebration at Passover. Easter has become a bland spring holiday for many, but the Seder celebration is full of meaning. When I was married I wanted to make sure my children appreciated the Jewish half of their heritage, so I carefully went through the Seder ceremony and rewrote the ritual in language they could understand when they were quite young. I updated the language when they reached middle childhood years and now they understand the adult version. It was good for me as well as them. I learned in the rewriting that it is a holiday that celebrates the ideal of the freedom and dignity of the human being. It also celebrates the renewal that comes with spring, and it pays homage to ancestors.

I want a holiday celebration like that for us gays, and I plan to stage one. It will have a meal with various foods being symbolic of the experiences of our gay ancestors. We will mourn our dead and pay tribute to their endurance. We will thank them for having made it possible for us to be here today in greater freedom than most of them experienced. I would like to blend into the ceremony some of the printed words of gay poets and writers, past and present. I would like to have a place in the ceremony where each person at the table can offer some personal thanks. Certainly there should be an empty place setting, like the glass of wine for Elijah, symbolizing that any gay person "out there" who needs us is welcome at our table. And there must be a game like hiding the matzoh. There must be at least one appropriate song that each of us can sing without worrying about how good our voice sounds. Maybe "Somewhere Over the Rainbow" would be sufficiently funny, touching and appropriately ironic. I would like the day to be an orgy of flowers, food, reflection, remembrance, thanks, affection, play and perhaps sex. Sex does seem appropriate for the historic release built into spring celebrations in many cultures, but our contemporary society is so wary and greedy about sex that we might have to ritualize it heavily and keep it tame to keep the guilts away. This is not a holiday where guilt is welcome. And what shall we call it? Maybe Appreciation Day.

I can imagine the faces of some non-gay aunts, uncles and cousins reading this and shaking their heads. Truthfully, I do not care if they understand. I spend a lot of my time and energy bridge-building between the gay and non-gay worlds.

If they do not understand the need for meaningful ceremony and celebration, too bad.

I am aware that many of us, perhaps most of us, are still too locked into tradition to break out and celebrate in these new ways, but I wish we all could. What a huge family we are, after all. And how wonderful it is to think of all of us in smaller family groupings, sometimes tiny family groupings, celebrating our holidays and developing our ceremonies. We must communicate about our new-found ways so that the new ceremonies can evolve.

How lovely to think that some non-gay people reading these words might want to join us in our celebrations and ceremonies. They might even get the idea of creating new rituals that better meet contemporary needs of non-gays.

4

Good Sports

I am starting to let myself feel happy sometimes. Not happy because of an accomplishment or happy in anticipation of an upcoming treat, but just happy to be me on a particular day or in a particular place. I can remember having glimpses of this happiness in the past: kneeling by the crib of my week-old daughter and staring into the wonder of her blue eyes as she wrapped a tiny hand around my thumb; or sneaking away from a useless and demoralizing work task one rainy, cold winter day at Fort Dix, New Jersey, and going into a PX to savor a hot cup of coffee and a jelly donut while my body thawed; sitting on a deserted beach in late September during high school years and feeling the peace and beauty; or having a quiet pretend time arranging "important papers" at a lamp table "desk" when I was a young child.

But these brief moments of happiness in the past would startle me and pass quickly from awareness, remembered because they had been so out of the ordinary and unexpected. My guess is that I assumed I did not deserve happiness because I was a bad person. After all, I was very much inter-

ested in male bodies, and in landscapes, colors, and tex-
tures—and not very interested in what I knew boys *should*
like: baseball games in the hot sun, fistfights, torturing in-
sects. I might have found the courage to defend my interest in
aesthetics, but I knew better than to even hint at my interest
in male bodies. So I felt myself to be different, wrong, and
bad through the first several decades of my life. And happiness is not granted to bad people; every story and movie I had
ever encountered assured me of that.

I suppose my surprise glimpses at unearned happiness
vanished from awareness so rapidly because consciousness
had caught me, like a thief, touching that which seemed not
meant for the likes of me, thereby adding to my sins in that
moment and reinforcing my self-concept as a bad person. I
know I have worked too hard most of my life at trying to do
good and I cannot remember any truly sinful actions,
thoughts, or fantasies (except my private gay identity) that
would prompt such massive atonement.

One of my newly allowed periods of happiness descended
on me while I was at my son's soccer game last week. While
they were practicing, the sun came out with stunning
warmth, changing what had been a damp, gray winter morning. I put the top down on my VW convertible, put on the
sunglasses that are a souvenir of a trip to France, and my
leather jacket that is a souvenir of a trip to London. I had
been reading *The Advocate* (a national gay newspaper—and
there was some good news in it for a change); it lay on the
seat beside me. I turned on the car radio and was swept into
the middle of the Brahms Double Concerto. My son's team
went onto the field and I realized my car was parked in such
a good location that I had a wonderful view right where I
was. My son smiled and waved at me and I waved back.
Happiness. It descended on me and stayed with me through
the entire Saturday.

Sitting in the car, I began to think how proud I am of my
son. When I say "my," I know he is not a possession and that
I did not create all that is wonderful about him. Part of what

I admire is his sunny disposition, which he blends with an alert, caring sensitivity to other people. Almost everyone is taken with him on first meeting and he puts effort into not abusing the privilege that comes with being so positively viewed by the world. And he is capable of doing things his own way, a little different, and not being terribly offended if some other child points it out or teases him. He knows already at age twelve that it is worthwhile to be an individual and that "different" does not mean "bad."

When he signed up for an American Youth Soccer Organization team four years ago, I had grave misgivings about how it would influence him. Less lethal than Little League baseball, it still contains the potential for grownups to batter children emotionally in a crazed attempt to right the injuries to pride and self-esteem remembered from their own childhood. When I drove him to his first practice he was excited but a little anxious, too. I said that if this was not the right team or the right sport there would be plenty of other things to try. I met his coach who, unasked, told me he was more interested in having the kids learn and enjoy soccer than in winning. Of course, the coach thereby won my heart immediately. During the season he was a wonderful contrast to the other coaches at Saturday games. The other coaches would scream directives and criticisms at the children, agonizing over possible defeat. But our coach would move along the sideline quietly calling, "Don't bunch up, Blues!" through a small megaphone, making sure each child got a chance to play the positions he desired. He was wonderful, and I wrote him a letter at the end of the season thanking him and expressing my admiration for his values and style. He invited all parents and the team members to a potluck picnic at the end of the season and suggested the mothers and fathers play a short game as the opposing team. To liven things up he gleefully decided he would play as a member of both teams simultaneously, the one wild card in the deck. For as long as parental breath held out it was a wonderful, batty, Alice-in-Wonderland game.

For the next two years my son was blessed by another human being for a coach. He worked them harder at learning the techniques of the game and cared more about winning, but preferred encouragement to criticism and rewarded teamwork while discouraging individual heroics. Now Andy is strong enough in himself to manage the usual screaming coach with quiet dignity.

Sitting in the sun, hearing Brahms accompany the game that happy Saturday, I had some stray thought about other games, how we use the concepts of game and sport in our society, what we say is their purpose and what they actually teach.

Just a few weeks before, I had been at another Saturday game, sitting on the grass watching the game and the spectators. There were a dozen other parents there, plus the coaches and assistant coaches. I felt out of place. There is something smug about an American suburb, so much easy presumption about how people will behave; and, while the code of right and wrong may be violated in private, it is unthinkable to challenge it in public.

Two couples had brought a tarp and all four were sitting on it. They seemed to be comfortable friends, maybe neighbors. Perhaps they grew up together in one of these suburbs. One of the women was leaning her head against the shoulder of her mate while the man of the second couple had his arm around his wife. It was an easy, sure, casual, public display of affection. Certainly our world needs it. But it made me feel shut out. What if my lover and I were to come to one of these games and lean affectionately against one another, or one of us casually put his arm around the other's waist, as we chatted with another couple? It happens all the time at gay gatherings. But the suburbs, if not the world, seem to belong to people with heterosexual orientation, and the overwhelming majority of them would be quite offended if my lover and I expressed our affection so easily in public, I am sure. What they do not know is that such smug, silent prohibitions make me angry and cause me to see their public display of affection as offensive. I know that is not the way I want it to go. I want good-spirited expression of public affection for all people. But the quiet oppression of my equal right to express equal feelings is turning me sour. It turns me away from the desire for an integrated world. I am more comfortable in the gay social world where I do not have to monitor myself.

At that same game, I heard an excited mother shout "Trip him, Ralph!" as she ran along the sideline. And a father whose son had missed a pass near the goal threw his coat to the ground with a loud groan of vexation or disgust that seemed to distract and frighten his son.

What is sport about, anyway? What is all the talk of learning to be part of a team and developing "good sportsmanship?" If the purpose of learning the cooperation of teamwork only serves the goal of defeating another team, we have not progressed far from the jungle—just become more cunning. I guess that should not surpise me in a world that uses war and other forms of violence in "manly" charades of problem-solving.

At least some children still know how to play. I see them at it most often when they are unaware of observing adults. They use imagination to create activity that has intrinsic fun while helping them learn understanding and acceptance of the world's complexity—using a trash pile of cartons to create a world to be explored, for instance. Most of us adults have forgotten how to play for simple pleasure. We play to *win*.

Going to the opera is one of my ways of playing. It is a fairly passive sport which fits nicely into my life as a writer and psychologist. The silly, touching, human dramas portrayed on the opera stage are real "plays." They exaggerate our sorrows and joys and touch our emotions with wonderful music, inspired voices, and visually thrilling scenes. Things often turn out badly, as they do in play, but that is part of the satisfaction. When the opera ends badly, we may shed tears for the hero or heroine who gave up life to honor love, but it reminds us to honor our own values and maintain integrity.

And, as in all play, the one who "died" returns to life to accept the thunderous applause of the grateful audience who were vicarious participants in the drama.

The Saturday that I noticed the two couples on the tarp, my lover and I joined two friends at the opera in San Francisco in the evening. It was *Un Ballo in Maschera*, and a truly inspired performance. The San Francisco Opera is usually a comfortable place for gay people. An old war horse of an opera often will get a new production with some camp humor tastefully livening a dull scene here or there. There are plenty of same-gender couples in the audience, so being gay is not experienced as an issue. *Ballo* is full of scenes we adults still need to play out. The attempt to laugh in the face of fate when a gypsy seer predicts death by "reading" the hand of a friend; an unexpected love for someone not available and the need to express it at a level that is acceptable and self-respecting; a husband's presumption that he not only has the right but also the duty to punish his wife severely for thoughts and feelings that do not conform to the code of the community; and the ability of a man to feel such love for a male friend that he throws his life away carelessly rather than face the possibility of hurting his friend.

The audience was wildly enthusiastic, and one could sense that the artists were inspired by one another's performances. Flowers were thrown to the soprano, who received them tearfully and graciously. A gay man ran down the aisle to throw a bouquet to the tenor, who caught it in mid-air to the applause of the standing, cheering audience. It would have to be a *gay* man, I thought. We have the courage to congratulate another man with flowers.

That wonderful moment of flowers flying into the tenor's outstretched hand and the applause for the catcher *and* the thrower was contrasted with a scene during the preceding intermission. We had arranged to meet our friends by the balustrade to have some Irish coffee. We moved toward one another with open arms, happy to see them and elated by the spirited production. Both of our friends are also male. As we embraced a man and woman standing three feet away exchanged a look of distaste and made a show of turning their backs to us. It was a small incident but it left its mark on a festive occasion. A gay man is applauded for throwing the flowers everyone knew the tenor deserved (though a "respectable" male could not have done it), but we are contemptuously dismissed when we show civilized appreciation for one another in public, even at the San Francisco Opera. Only warriors of the football field who had just dealt a death blow to their male enemies would be permitted such a high-spirited show of affection and appreciation for one another. Those small reminders of society's rules pop up all the time, of course. How many times has each of us who is gay seen a lover or friend off on a trip, or welcomed him or her home after a lonely separation, and, because it happens in a public place like an airport, experienced an unfair feeling of constraint even if the conscious decision to kiss or embrace is made and acted upon. This most commonplace, everyday form of oppression is difficult for non-gay people to understand on an emotional level since they never experience it.

It does have to do with the idea of good sportsmanship, I think. In our society we pay lip service to the ideal that if you exercise your unique potential to its fullest, you deserve respect and praise. In a game you are expected to extend yourself. You must put out every ounce of skill, desire and energy you possess. And if a person on the other team does this you are expected to have the appreciation and innate good sportsmanship to offer genuine congratulations.

Maybe we can become a society of good sports. Certainly we have a lot of relearning to do first. We would have to stretch enough to appreciate a person's use of individual abilities and see how unimportant it is whether or not those abilities fit some code-prescribed form such as suitably "masculine" or "feminine" behavior. We would have to be able to applaud the man who tossed the bouquet to the tenor because he went beyond his usual limitations in order to do something that expressed everyone's feelings.

I think of the soccer game on the happy day when the sun came out and Brahms spoke to me from his unique spirit. He has been dead a long time, but his perceptive musical statements continue to move us. I want to applaud and shout "bravo" and thank him for not being limited to the code of his musical predecessors. And I remember the coach of the other team that day. He was a big, muscular man whose body language was a caricature of what we call masculine. His stance was so sturdy and solid that it was devoid of grace or fluidity. It looked as if he could neither stand nor move with ease. I would like to see him do something spontaneous from his innermost feelings and transcend the code he has learned at such a cost.

Maybe some day the disapproving couple at the opera will be able to say "bravo" to our willingness to express publicly a difference that is loving, kind and gentle. Maybe they will recognize that our release from bondage signals a freedom in which *they* can find new ways of expressing positive feelings toward other humans. Somehow the notion of good sportsmanship has gotten lost in our desire to compete and win. No one can really win in a society where conquest is a primary value. We have lost the fun of playing together and letting the play express us and move us to new levels of ability. We have lost the wonderfully inventive idea of a team that is greater than the sum of its members because a variety of truly individual talents complement one another and create new abilities. If we can recapture our appreciation of individual differences, we may be able to recapture good sportsmanship.

I am going to continue to let myself have more happy times because I know better each day that I am "different" but not "bad" and do not need to punish myself by being unhappy. Sitting in the car that day, I saw my son wave to me and saw another boy imitate his left-handed wave as a derisive reinforcement of conformity to the "boy-code." My son looked at him blankly for a moment and then turned in my direction to smile and wave again. He also does a brief celebratory dance on the field sometimes when something happens that pleases him. It looks odd, individual. It also looks like fun and it seems to express his feelings and add to the joy of his life.

I know there have been at least a couple of times in the past when he has been called upon to explain his father since I am public about being different. It has seemed relatively easy for him to explain that I am gay. I think he knows that no apologies are due but he can also appreciate the person's curiosity. I think he is conscious of differences in people and has learned to appreciate it when anyone exercises these differences in a manner that transcends the mundane and adds positive variety to the world. He is enjoying the world and he really is a good sport.

5

Invisible Children

It is the troubled, unhappy children that bother me most, setting off feelings of impotent rage and despair in me when our eyes meet. I see them in supermarkets, elevators, birthday parties and classrooms. Sometimes the child is seven, sometimes seventeen. I recognize the quiet misery in their eyes most easily when it is a boy, because I can draw on my own experience as well as the experiences described to me by so many friends and clients. But I am sure I see it sometimes in the eyes of a girl and the pain is the same.

Last month, my children and I flew to Hawaii to break the gray spell of winter. On the plane, a girl of nine or ten sat with her parents one row ahead of us and across the aisle. Her parents were in their thirties, well-dressed and pleasantly involved with one another, chatting over drinks and macadamia nuts. The girl first caught my attention when she asked to change seats with her father, from the window to the aisle. I began to watch her. One particular stewardess was extremely attractive and pleasant as she hurried about her duties. The girl's eyes were on her constantly, while a comic book lay unread in her lap. The stewardess was doing one thing that was subtly different. Everytime she passed the other stewardesses she would touch them affectionately and smile directly into their eyes. The young girl seemed hypnotized. Then the stewardess noticed her rapt attention, bent down and touched the girl's arm and asked if she wanted anything. The girl blushed, shook her head and pretended great interest in the comic book.

Then came the event that shifted my perception of her behavior from schoolgirl infatuation with a role model and activated my inner sense of knowing, with its consequent agony. The girl's mother, drawn by some parental instinct, suddenly broke off her spirited conversation with her husband in the middle of a laugh, turned to her daughter, who seemed engrossed in the comic book, and said sharply "What's the matter with you?" The child looked instantly guilty and startled as her head moved closer to her shoulders and she slumped slightly in her seat. "Nothing," she answered, darting a guarded look in her mother's direction. Her mother squirmed uneasily in her seat, seemingly bothered by something that had slipped her mind, then returned her attention to the conversation with her husband. After a few more seconds with the comic book, the girl glanced cautiously around, as if to see if anyone was watching, then her eyes searched until they located the stewardess again.

That child was experiencing gay feelings. She was also experiencing guilt and shame. Her mother is subliminally bothered and angered by something in her daughter that does not feel normal. The girl senses her mother's discomfort and will do her best to hide the feelings that presumably are wrong. But she is irresistibly attracted to the stewardess who bodily shows her affection to other women. The child is left to puzzle out the confusion in her loneliness. The answer will come out as it always does, a growing inner conviction that "I am different and that difference makes me bad." She may hide the festering infection of self-concept from others by becoming a model child who does everything right. She may be successful in sending the painful doubts about her self-worth out of conscious awareness, but even then a nagging sense of justice will cause her to sabotage her own attempts to reach out for happiness. The inner judge (superego) will render the verdict silently: "Since you are basically a bad and defective person you are not entitled to happiness and must not contaminate others by trying to make intimate contact with them; you are to continue a life of private loneliness in which you work every day to help make the world a better place for *normal* people who deserve happiness."

Sometimes the interaction between adults and children that facilitates this sad slaughter of self-respect is not so subtle. Since I am a publicly gay person, I rarely see the blatant adult destruction of gay children. The adults feel awkward and perhaps guilty when I am present. But I continue to hear about it.

A client whom I shall call Jeff came to me saying that, though he was a heterosexual, he had met me socially and knew intuitively I was the right person to help him. He wanted to discover why he stopped himself from finding any peace and harmony in the world and how he could reach out to others with love. During eighteen months of searching, he recalled long-forgotten examples of the hundreds of times he had violently rejected gay feelings and tried to force their replacement with heterosexual feelings. He looks and feels better now, breathes more easily, and has more self-acceptance and appreciation for *all* of his feelings.

Last month Jeff came to my office with a headache, feeling tight, unable to identify what had happened in the preceding twenty-four hours that had set off this internal storm. As we searched and sorted, it turned out that he had had dinner at the home of friends. Jeff had been close to their children for the past half dozen years, going along on trips to the beach, shooting baskets and backpacking with the oldest boy, now in his early teens.

During the dinner, this oldest son talked enthusiastically about how Michael, a young man who was another friend of the family, might soon be able to offer him an after-school job. The mother, a well-educated, kind, socially active, intelligent and usually sensitive person, said, "You two have been spending a lot of time together. Michael's not queer, is he?" It was a little joke, said casually and with a smile. She was voicing a mild uneasiness and did not really believe it could be founded in fact.

Jeff was dumbstruck. Awareness and acceptance of his own gay feelings being relatively recent, he had not yet discussed them with these friends. He was horrified at the casual anti-gay remark from this tolerant woman. "She's even been on the Board of the ACLU!" he said. He was hurt and frightened by his invisibility to them. He left as soon as gracefully possible and went home to write it out in his journal. He had seen what he must do to clear the air with his friends and knew how he would handle the disclosure of his identity as well as his feelings about the dinner incident.

During our session together, Jeff discovered why he was feeling the emotional logjam even after having clarified things so well. A year earlier, before admitting his gay feelings to awareness, Jeff had gone backpacking with the oldest boy from this family. They had shared confidences, as people do in the quiet wilderness. Jeff had forgotten that the boy had confessed that he felt troubled because he had been attracted to other boys for years and suspected himself to be a homosexual; the boy feared that other people, particularly his family, would find out and not want to be around him anymore. He had found the courage to end his admission with the revelation that he was also attracted to Jeff.

Jeff burst into tears in my office. "He was sitting right there at the goddamned dining room table and I saw his eyes when his mother said it. She was smiling at the roast as she carved it and she didn't miss a goddamned stroke. The words came out of her mouth and she didn't *look* at him!" Jeff hit his leg with clenched fist, covering his own eyes as if to stop the vision. His voice was choked with tears. "His eyes looked like he knew it had been coming, like he was accepting death. She

might as well have put the carving knife right through him."
Jeff cried quietly for some minutes. His headache and the
tight feeling were gone. He remembered his own mother
making similar casual remarks. He wanted to rush to the boy
and try to ease his pain. He wanted to share his own evolving
awareness that one can be gay and good, though the world is
not always fair.

"And I am pissed!" Jeff said, looking out into the garden.
"When I tell them about my own gay feelings they are not going to trust me alone with their son anymore. I know it." His
face appeared tired as he turned and looked at me. "Why do
decent people keep this nightmare going?" he asked. "Now
when I can be of some real help to him at last, they're going
to let him know he shouldn't trust me. I don't want to hurt
him. I don't want to have sex with him. I just want to help
him avoid some wasted years."

Invisibility can be deadly. The most frequently used estimate of the gay population of this country is 10 percent,
though most gay professionals would say it is higher. Using
the 10 percent estimate, a classroom of thirty children probably has two to four gay youngsters in it. A town with thirty
thousand children has three thousand gay children. They are
an invisible minority who are receiving daily messages indi-
cating at best, that gay is not as good as heterosexual; at
worst, that gay is sick, evil and deserving of punishment.
These messages are dangerous to their developing self-images
and pose a national mental health problem of staggering
proportions, since it is not only the developing gay people
who are injured, but also their families.

The most sensible place to intervene in this tragic cycle of
emotional battering is in the schools. I am not sufficiently
naive to believe that any teacher training program could re-
verse the centuries of bigotry and prejudice present in the
average teacher, any more than I expect it to be reversed in
the next decade in the average citizen. But I believe that the
more enlightened and least prejudiced citizens can be
reached, and that their basic decency will force them to sup-

port programs aimed at giving gay youngsters a better chance of survival.

Our best hope is to support teachers who are able and willing to make their gay identity public. Again, chances are that more than one out of ten teachers is gay. If only one out of ten is public about being gay and can demonstrate a life as self-respecting as that of most other teachers, what a wonderful support it would be for the invisible gay youngsters in the classroom.

The coalition of the self-righteous and the fascists who chose Dade County as a testing ground in their crusade against full citizenship rights for gay people, shrewdly hit a sensitive nerve in the voting public by charging that homosexual teachers would "recruit" the young "because they cannot reproduce." This simple-minded belief ignores the court battles being waged by gay parents who are trying to maintain contact with the children produced of their flesh. It pretends that there are relatively few gay teachers. It ignores that fact that gay people have been fine educators since before Socrates and Plato, who were as gay as they were outstanding educators. It is a simple message of evil designed to keep teachers in the closet for fear of loss of employment and public humiliation. If their strategy succeeds, gay youngsters will continue to grow up invisible, believing that no gay person can hold such a respectable position in the community as that of a teacher. And, of course, these bigots would then move on to point to elected officials, lawyers, doctors, newspaper reporters and others as people who also wield influence and might "recruit" the young into the terrible homosexual world. It does not take too much imagination to see how that strategy can eventually eliminate anyone who opposes its leaders. Dictatorships grow from these seeds. It is not only in the interest of gay youngsters and their families, but also in the national interest, that we *at least* consistently oppose the harassment of gay teachers.

An articulate but little-known poet, Tom Savignano, wrote a poem entitled *Teachers First* in response to a newspaper article under the headline "Gay Teacher Loses Appeal to High Court." The first four paragraphs of the article read:

Washington

The U.S. Supreme Court yesterday let stand rulings by state courts in Washington that homosexuals are "immoral" and may be fired from their jobs because of their sexual preference.

The nation's highest court refused to hear the appeal of a Tacoma, Wash., high school social studies teacher who was fired after nearly 13 years on the job because he acknowledged being a homosexual.

Civil liberties attorneys representing James Gaylord had hoped his case would be used as a vehicle by the court to break new legal ground. The court has not dealt with the rights of homosexuals since 1967.

Gaylord taught at Tacoma's Wilson High School until 1972, when school officials learned of his homosexuality. Although no misconduct involving other faculty members or students was alleged, Gaylord was fired for violating the school district's rule against immorality.

Savignano's poem:

TEACHERS FIRST

hide, you gays,
and be silent,
tell lies if you have to

don't make a spectacle of yourselves

subdue your flagrant spirits,
fold up your blossoms

we are laying concrete down around our schools
so our kids can play and be safe
from wonder

we are expanding our moral parking lots
for these young impressionable souls

listen, pansies,
we are afraid of you

we know that seeds have a way
of settling in cracks
and sending down their roots

we know that grass
quietly subtly
defeats concrete

all grass and flowers must be strictly sequestered
to keep our schoolyards suitable

so cooperate, gays,
lie back and let the referendums roll

help us safeguard our stainless
American institutions

help us Save Our Children
from styrofoam womb to styrofoam tomb

drop your banners, dismantle your floats,
you proud cocky gays

we're afraid of you
help us
not to be afraid

be good gays
and hide

What we need as a modest plan to begin to support gay youngsters is an affirmative action program in the employment of gay teachers. Many gay teachers have been so frightened by harassment campaigns that they will need in-service training courses to help them learn more about themselves as gay people. They need access to gay history, gay psychology, gay culture and gay consciousness-raising. And such supportive programs should be made available as they have been for black teachers.

But that takes time. Meanwhile, we will have to depend on the brave, spirited and dedicated teachers who have already revealed their gay identity and those on the verge of doing so if they can be assured they will not lose employment.

It boggles my mind to realize that one out of ten of my teachers over the years was gay. If only one teacher at the Belmar Grammar School or one teacher in the Asbury Park High School (just sixty miles from the cosmopolitan city of New York), had been able to live in public peace with a life partner of the same gender, how much easier and less painful my life would have been!

In college, I remember two male faculty members being whispered about as "queer" but they were each in "the arts" which was viewed as unimportant and therefore harmless and acceptable. Now if the college president had been openly gay he would have been asked to resign—even though it was Antioch College, bastion of civil rights. We picketed the local barber shop that would not cut the hair of "colored folks," and I danced with a black coed in the coffee shop, but queers were out.

And in graduate school the professor from whom I learned the most told me he was gay five years after I made my first announcement and ten years after I left graduate school. If I had known he was gay when he was my teacher it could have changed my life. But it was not safe and in many institutions continues not to be safe to make any public announcement of gay identity. You may not get promotions and tenure. You may find your contract has not been renewed. Does anyone seriously believe that gay teachers might do a fraction of the job of promoting homosexuality that non-gay teachers do in promoting heterosexuality? And they wonder why I do not contribute money to my alma mater! When they start supporting gay students and teachers, I will gladly support the schools.

Another need that will be served when more gay teachers are visible is that children who know a parent is gay will be able to see other responsible gay adults, not only the gay parent and his or her friends. As a gay parent I am aware that my children have to take a lot on faith. They know me and my gay friends, but they do not hear directly about many public figures who are gay. Once in a while they find something in a newspaper, but it is rarely good news about gay people. Several of their teachers over the years have confided gay identity to me, but felt they dared not let it be known publicly. Too bad. In every case, it was a teacher who was especially loved and respected.

I was sitting in on a staff meeting at their school once when an assisting teacher made her disclosure to the staff in a wonderful way. There had been whisperings about her and another woman teacher and she decided she had nothing to lose by meeting rumor and innuendo head on. She was leaving in a few months for a different kind of employment anyway. She said, "For those of you who are wondering, I would like you to know that I *am* gay. I would also like you to know that if it takes you a few weeks or months to get used to it, that's okay with me because it took me *years* to get used to it." When she asked if anyone had any response, I had to tell her that I thought she was a beautiful person but I did have a complaint. She had been teaching my son that year; he thought she was wonderful and because of her an interest in words and language had been kindled in him. But, I thought he had been cheated out of some learning as well as some reassurance by not knowing and having his friends know she was gay.

Since I am a parent, people ask sometimes how *I* would feel if one of my own children were homosexually molested by a trusted adult such as a teacher. The repetition has dulled my surprise at the question, though it still causes me to look more closely at the questioner and the probable prejudice behind the unspoken presumption.

The answer is that I would not like my children to be molested, sexually or otherwise, by homosexual or heterosexual intent, by a trusted adult or a teenage stranger. Ironically, the hysteria about possible homosexual molestation completely ignores the facts that homosexual contact outside of prisons is so likely to be by consent of both parties that an exception is extremely rare—which cannot be said of heterosexual contacts; and 90 percent of child molesters are heterosexual, most of them relatives of the victim. Knowing the facts, I find it a weird question. I am aware that my children, like everyone's children, will have some sexual experiences or overtures less pleasant than others. I hope they know already how to say, "Thanks but no thanks," when the offer is undesirable, whether its intent is homosexual or heterosexual. Gay people are not intent on "recruiting" youngsters to "our way" as straight heterosexuals often do. We need to be visible as teachers so that we can protect gay youngsters from an abusive environment and help to rebuild the self-esteem of those gay children who have been damaged.

Of course, it is not only visible gay teachers that we need as potential role models for gay children. This year I have been involved in a plan that would have seemed wildly impossible to me ten years ago. A number of sturdy gay activists in San Francisco (due to the laudable and persistent urging of one man who cared enough to prod the rest of us) have worked at seeing to it that there would be a respectable number of gay women and men applying for the civil service examinations to become members of the city police force. The Chief of Police had made a public request that members of all minority groups in the city, including gay people, apply, and had gone on to urge that gay members of the force be open in their gay identity. At one evening meeting, as I faced approximately sixty gay women and men who were considering the daring move, I told them that I was impressed as always by the courage of pioneers. But I was most moved and grateful to know some of them would become uniformed police officers with a genuine sense of justice and reasoned law enforcement, visible individuals to whom untold numbers of gay

youngsters could look with pride and thanks for helping them
to develop a sense of worth and respectability.

We need to face the problem of gay children who are in
need of family placement. Whether because of death or parental unwillingness and/or inability to assume sufficient responsibility, some children each year become the wards of
the state. Ten percent of them are gay. There is a multitude of
willing and able gay people to do the parenting and provide
solid families if they are permitted to do so. Some agencies
have already discovered that single gay people can be wonderful foster and adoptive parents to children who are non-
gay, gay, or undetermined. Prospective gay foster and adoptive parents must be screened and selected as carefully as
non-gay propective parents, of course, but the gay parents
who qualify tend more often to be parents who listen carefully to a youngster's growing pains and know how hard it is to
feel loved for being your real self. Nor need anyone fret about
gay parents forcing their wards to be gay. Straight parents
have been siring and raising gay youngsters for thousands of
years and all evidence to date suggests that gay parents are
equally able to raise straight youngsters and, on the average,
be far less resentful of the difference in sexual orientation.

But what a possible boon to gay children if they are more
consistently placed in the homes of gay parents! The world
may continue to be unkind but there would be a family behind them who really understood their feelings and stood
ready to give active parental support in word and deed.

While agencies have been placing youngsters with single
gay parents, they are still reluctant to place them with gay
couples. This is another manifestation of lingering homophobia, reflecting fear that a gay couple may actually have
sex together and therefore be a bad influence. The fear does
not stand up to the light of reason so, as usual, it is ration-
alized and disguised. The implication is that gay parents are
good parents if they stay in the closet (in their place) and do
not get public or uppity. Well, we have been through all that
already with countless minority groups, most recently blacks

and women. Let us hope it will pass and be replaced with
sanity. Secure foster and adoptive homes of gay parents for
gay children is a precious opportunity for alchemy; double
tragedy could be forged in the furnace of loving care and
produce the gold of harmony, self-respect and self-assurance.

There is so much that needs to be done to help invisible gay
children and their families. Positive programs in the schools
for children and teachers will make it safe for more gay children to choose some degree of visibility. Truly sensitive, gay-
oriented counselors in the schools would help a lot too.

As we find ways to help gay children attain safety in visibility, we must also find ways to help their families understand the gay experience and not let the training of an ignor-
ant society poison their relationships with their gay offspring.

6

Some Parents Can't

There are so many different opinions about what parents should be and what they should do. The title of this chapter is a reminder to me as well as to readers that some parents *can't*, for a variety of reasons.

In the newspapers these days one can find stories of legal battles being waged in courts by mothers who happen to be lesbians and who are being deprived of parental rights for that reason alone. They want to be good parents but they can't, because a judge will not let them.

There are fewer stories of gay fathers waging legal battles in custody issues because tradition dictates that when in doubt, the mother gets custody. If the father is gay in addition to being male, he can pretty well count on kissing his children goodbye if a legal fight starts. He may very well want desperately to be a good parent, but he can't.

And some non-gay parents would like to be good parents to their gay offspring. When a person discloses gay identity to a parent, it is almost always in the hope of ending secrets and strengthening the parent-child bond. Parents often cry and feel wounded, wondering how they can deal with this tragedy—forgetting that their child, having much less experience in weathering life's storms, has had to deal with it alone, suffering in secret silence, and now offers to help them learn that the presumed "tragedy" can become an easy, even happy, fact of life. These parents who have been blinded by too many years of prejudice would like to be good parents, but they can't.

And some people just do not have what it takes to be a good parent. They believe the romantic mystique of parenthood portrayed in soft focus in films. They prove themselves biologically capable of creating a baby and then learn that it is too consuming a responsibility, lacks glamour, and robs them of the attention they still need. This can happen whether a parent is gay or non-gay. We would do well to help such parents find graceful, socially acceptable ways of turning the parenting over to someone who is ready for it and can enjoy it. It would make for many fewer unhappy homes and save countless children who are being battered emotionally and physically.

But lots of parents, gay and non-gay, *can.* They know intuitively and from experience that a youngster grows best in the warmth of unconditional love, the air of trust, and the light of truth. Parental manipulation, guilt induction, and a family full of secrets produce kinks and scars.

Some people fret about whether a gay father can adequately parent a daughter, or whether a gay woman can do the same for a son. "What about sex role identity," they ask, forgetting what a mess rigid sex roles have produced in this society, creating a population of half-selves who say, "You can't sew because you're male and you mustn't build roads because you're female."

I want my daughter to grow up to be a *person*, proud of her breasts and vagina, as I hope my son as a person will be proud of his penis, but well aware that anatomy must not be allowed to limit gifts that can be developed in an evolving, satisfying life. A youngster needs loving access to both parents when it is possible, not to reinforce silly sex roles, but to learn the ways he or she can be loved by two such different people. The child needs permission to be, not prohibition.

Some people also worry about gay parents turning indecisive children gay. Such parental power is no match for that of the culture that tirelessly promotes heterosexuality. I know scores of gay parents and only three with gay offspring.

Being gay has helped me to see clearly how people who need to be good parents transcend great obstacles to do so. I think, for instance, of the Parents of Gay People organization and the often-quoted statement of one of its founders, Sarah Montgomery: "I refuse to be a closet mother." Gay Fathers and Lesbian Mothers groups are also rapidly proliferating around the country.

Perhaps I should say something about my own efforts to be a good parent. I have written two open letters to my children. The first was prepared for my part of a panel presentation entitled *Gay Parents and Parents of Gays* at the 1974 meeting of the Association of Humanistic Psychology. The second was written as a contribution to a book entitled, *Positively Gay*, edited by Betty Berzon and Robert Leighton, and published by Celestial Arts in 1979. Together, the letters reveal my changes and constancies as a parent who is gay:

August 1974

Dear Vicki and Andy,

This letter is for you but I am writing it in more grown-up language than I would use with you today when you are seven and nine years old. The reason is that I have another purpose for writing it. Many grown-ups are curious about what it is like to be gay and to be a father. Some of them have a hard time understanding that it is possible to be both gay and a father. So this letter is written to share some of my thoughts, feelings, and experiences with them and to be saved for you to read when you are older because I think you will find it interesting then too.

There are no secrets in this letter but there are some thoughts that might frighten you today—I hope unnecessarily. Only these frightening thoughts have I withheld from you. The rest I have shared in language that you can understand. I know that you do not fully comprehend what it means to be gay, but I think you understand it about as well as you understand what it means to be Jewish.

Our world is filled with fear of people who are different. The nice word for such people is *nonconformist*, the not so nice word is *deviant*. That deviant has an unpleasant ring tells the story. The word indicates a deviation from the norm, statistical mean, or average. We are uncomfortable about events and people who are not average. Our society's fear of the different cheats us of the richness that would be available in our community if we were to encourage differences. It also leads to atrocities that more open civilizations would view with distaste.

There was a time when the fairest youths were given by their parents to be thrown into the fiery depths of an active volcano in pious fear of the god who supposedly lived therein. They hoped that the sacrifice of their children would appease the god and save lives and crops in the community. Our cruel god today is not a volcano; it is the god of conformity. We sacrifice our fairest, wisest, and most gifted to it. Parents sometimes disown a daughter or son who is gay. When the fear of nonconformity climbs to hysteria, whole groups are sacrificed, as when Americans of Japanese ancestry were rounded up, stripped of their life's possessions and their human rights, and put in barbed-wire-enclosed concentration camps in this country. At any time, a talented priest of the god of conformity, someone like our once-revered Senator Joseph McCarthy, can point the accusing finger of nonconformity by calling someone a deviant name such as *communist* or *homosexual* and strip that person of community respect, livelihood, freedom and possibly even life itself.

I know that these things can happen. This is the kind of fearful thought that I am withholding from you, Vicki and Andy. Homosexuals provide an easy target group for prosecution. The high priests of conformity like to use us to whip public fear into hysteria because we are not visible. If gay people do not speak or behave their truth, they cannot be identified. Priests of conformity love to trade on this idea that the criminal could be anyone—a neighbor, friend, or even a relative. Traditionally, for instance, big city politicians produce a publicized crackdown on homosexuals just before a major election. It fills the front pages of newspapers and diverts attention from seemingly less urgent items such as how these politicians have been using public funds and public trust.

It could happen one day that our priests might whip up a wave of profound hysteria and, explaining the regrettable danger of having subversive homosexuals loose in the community, fill concentration camps with identified and supposedly gay people. If that were to happen, I would do my best to escape detention but I would, almost surely, be separated from you. I will try my best not to let this happen. My visibility as a gay person, my writing, public speaking, and this open letter are an attempt to make it less likely that it will ever happen.

You two, Vicki and Andy, are more important to me than my own life. It is a flat-sounding statement, but true. Remember the last summer vacation that we spent on Long Beach Island? I am thinking of the time when we three went to the beach and the two of you went into the water. The tide began to carry you out before anyone realized what was happening. You were too frightened at the time to notice, but I was only a little surprised to find that my instinct was to preserve your lives at all cost. I had already gotten you into shallow water, Andy, and had gone back for you, Vicki. At one moment I felt myself going under the water, pulled by the tide, and my one impulse was to find enough footing to keep your head above water and keep somehow pushing you toward the shore.

I carry half the responsibility for having given you each a start at life and I continue to carry the responsibility for helping you to build your own lives. I believe, as your father, that I owe you truth. I have told you that I will never knowingly lie to you and I mean it. It is my job to tell you the truth, as I understand it, and respect your attempts to find your own truth.

Part of my motivation in being openly gay is to further my own growth. But another part is to provide a model for you. I want each of you to see that you have the right to be yourself and speak your own truth aloud. It is not an accident that I began to be more open about my gayness after you were born. It was partly the flavor of the times. Black people were teaching us how to throw off oppression with nonviolent dignity and many of us were marching in the streets to protest the immorality of war. Those things helped. But it was holding you in the June sunlight, Vicki, and watching you delight in the beginning of each new day, Andy, that made me look into your trusting eyes and wonder what sort of lives the world would permit you to have.

Such thinking helped me to understand that oppression and restriction thrive on the cooperation of the victim. I began to understand that if I wanted a wide world of possibilities for you, I had better start doing what I could to build such a world. The first and most urgent personal step was to become truthful and visible in my gayness.

As you grow up, people may tell you that I am sick, immoral, or that I use you kids and Mom as a shield to hide behind. I know that hearing these things may hurt you. I hope that you will not be bullied. I hope that in thinking about these things your understanding will grow and you will become stronger. I have read everything that I can about homosexuality and gayness. I have read as a trained social scientist; I have also read with the understanding based on my own life experiences. I believe the charge that homosexuality is a sickness is a lie. It is based on the naive assumption that normality equals mental health and that the true norm of human behavior is synonymous with the *current mode* of behavior and feelings to which the masses are encouraged to conform.

Nor do I believe that I am immoral. I am speaking my truth even when it is uncomfortable and dangerous. I believe that is being moral. Being gay means that I can view other men as possible loved ones. I am capable of sexual, emotional, and spiritual attraction to another man. This means that I reject my culture's training to compete and kill other men in commerce and war so as to support the power of my masters. In rejecting the prescribed masculine role and accepting myself as a potential lover of another man, I believe that I am moral. I offer my hand to build rather than to destroy.

As to using the two of you and Mom for a shield, your experience is sufficient to show the untruth of this. You've heard Mom and me reminisce about our years together since we met at age 17. Our nine years of friendship before we married helped us to get to know one another well. It provided the truth and mutual respect that are the foundations of our profound love for one another. You have shared many of our sorrows, joys, anger, frustrations, and moments of quiet appreciation. If, from your own experience, you wonder why someone would imply that there is dishonesty in my love for the three of you, consider once more the fear that is generated by nonconformity.

Many people, both straight and gay, have accepted the notion that there are two kinds of people. They believe that you must choose from Column A or Column B. They ignore the truth that life, like any truly great restaurant, offers its best delights to the discriminating who dare order a

la carte. All the data from respectable social science research supports the view that human nature is a matter of
continua rather than a matter of categories. But the myth
of gay vs. straight continues. Since I have chosen a satisfying straight lifestyle and yet am admittedly gay, I do not
conform to the myth of categories. As a nonconformist I
am anxiety-provoking and therefore viewed with distrust
by some people. When people are fearful, they are apt to
strike out. By now you know that this is what provokes
most of the teasing on the playground.

When people strike out at you by saying nasty things
about me, try to remember that they are afraid. Their fear
makes them irrational. Treat them as you would anyone
who is irrational. Be wary and take care not to provoke
them. But also understand that what they are saying is not
of any importance. The time to engage in dialogue with
them is when they are back in their right senses. Treat
them with tolerance and patience meanwhile, but do not
permit them to molest you or harm you in any way. If
necessary, use the superior strength of your sober truth and
rational sense to hold them at arm's length or leave them
to their own ugliness for the time being and come back to
them another day, when security has sobered them once
more.

I hope that both of you choose carefully the individuals
you love. I hope that you permit yourselves to enjoy the
widest range of attractions possible. I hope that you are
not restricted in taste by skin color, politics, gender, or
language. But I hope that while permitting yourselves the
widest possible range of attractions, you become terribly
selective in finding the individuals with whom you choose
to share love and friendship. Look for the persons with
whom you can share in ways that help you both to grow
in understanding, depth of feeling, appreciation, and respect. Beware the programming of our culture that would
lead you to believe that visual appearance can equal beauty. Waistline, age, teeth, and eyelashes have little to do

with the beauty of love or even with the possible shared fun of recreational sex.

I hope that each of you will find the courage to speak your truth aloud, as you find it. I hope that you will never strike out to hurt anyone whose truth is different than yours. Destroying property and lives can call attention to your cause but ultimately it generates more fear. If you find the courage to speak your truth aloud consistently, and let others with opposing truths speak theirs aloud, while refusing to support the oppression of yourself or others, the decades and centuries will decide the ultimate truths. It takes the courage of the child who said the Emperor was naked. It takes remembering that striking out against the truth of someone else can rob our world of someone like Martin Luther King.

I am gay. I am your father. I hope to be permitted to watch your lives unfold. If this imperfect world should somehow separate me from you, know that I will have lost the most precious gift that life has granted me. Know also that I am aware of your love for me and Mom's love for me. I know that I will be with you always because I am built into your flesh and we have had wonderful years to-gether. Thank you for being yourselves. And thank you for helping me to find myself.

* * * * *

October 1977

Dear Vicki and Andy,

Now it is three years and two months later. Some things have changed and some remain the same. Perhaps that is one way to trace truth, seeing what remains true through time.

You are twelve and eleven years old now. Your mother and I separated 21 months ago and you live half time with me and half time with her. We have all weathered the worst of that trauma in our lives, though the death of marriage and the snug nuclear family will be mourned the way any important death is mourned for years to come.

Do you know what gave me the courage to say the words aloud and acknowledge that I truly did not want to be married any more? I took a long walk on the beach one day when we were all there together and I sat and looked into the ocean for a long time. I admitted to myself that I was done with marriage (not done with your mother or with you), and that I was hanging on to the *form* of marriage in the most pleasant ways possible because I wanted you to have that kind of storybook family during your growing-up years.

I knew better. As a psychologist I had pointed out the error of that kind of thinking for years to other people. It usually leads to resentment all around, hidden lies, and deep unhappiness for parents and children. I imagined how it would hurt the two of you to have the words spoken aloud and the pain that would come with the actual separation of your parents. And then another truth descended on me. I remembered that the most precious gift that I can give you is to have you see me live my life openly so that you can see options that are open to you as you grow older. I realized that to stay in a marriage that had died for me would too easily be seen as middle-aged insecurity—hanging in there for fear of taking those risks that provide opportunity to grow but also provide the chance of hurt, disappointment, and pain. I knew, as I know today, that the law of life is "grow or die." I knew I wanted to keep growing. And I realized that I wanted to *show* you rather than just *tell* you that it is possible to take growth risks even in middle age, survive the pain, and grow more into the person you can become. Within a week of that realization I plunged into the turmoil that accompanies such a major change in life.

I know that today you miss some of the times we had as a family together. So do I. But I also know, because you have told me and because I can see it, that all four of us are freer of tension and all four of us are much more clearly developing our individual lives. It has had a price but we are growing.

And that brings me to a major point that did not ring true as I read the letter I wrote to you three years ago. I made a point of telling you that your lives were more important to me than my own. Your lives are very important to me *and* so is my own. The big thing I have learned is that unless I live my own life the best way I know how, getting as much out of it as possible, growing every year until I die, tending it as I would a garden to bring out its beauty, I cannot complete my parental responsibility in giving you your own individual lives. If I stay locked into presumed responsibilities to you or other people, and use those presumed responsibilities to divert my energy and retard my growth, I will be resentful and I will have demonstrated beyond any words I may speak to the contrary that the true purpose of life is to serve others through self-denial. If I ever believed that, I no longer do. I do not want to see the two of you grow up into lives where you follow some cultural script that says you must play out certain responsible and respectable roles at the cost of your own flowering.

This leads us into complex areas of philosophy. I know you and trust you as I do myself. I know you would not willingly harm another person. I know that you will honor your love relationships and do what you can to help those you love. But you do not help those you love by sacrificing your own identity.

I am not sure I would have been able to work my way to this truth had I not been gay. I see so many non-gay friends locked into roles that are not satisfying and, rather than dare to break the mold of the roles, they struggle to carry the burden—and I can see the beauty of their individuality and spontaneity die day by day. But I had to face it. The day I admitted to myself and others that my truth was "different," I could no longer fit into any culturally prescribed role exactly. I admitted that I was gay—a man capable of sharing sexual, emotional, and intellectual love with other males. I could still compete against other men, but not with the abandon of a man who is not aware of that kind of love potential within himself. I never had cared for the mandate to compete and kill that I received in this society, presented nakedly in the Army. Once an admitted gay, I had to find slightly different ways of relating to my fellow male. And I had to find new ways of relating to women. I was forced to see them as more than sexual objects or housewives before such altered perceptions were fashionable.

And perhaps most pertinent for this letter, I had to find new ways of being a father because I was gay. Many gay fathers feel forced to hide their truth, but I knew you and I would be better off in the long run if we did not have lies between us. I wanted to find ways of being that would make you proud of me, but I knew they would have to be different ways.

I have seen that struggle come to fruition in the past few years. I have seen the pride in your eyes when you introduce me or my gay friends to friends of yours. I have heard the pride with which you are able to speak about my being gay with your friends in an easy and natural tone of voice while they are tempted to whisper or be embarrassed. When my book was published earlier this year, you went with me to the first TV taping of an interview and also to the first newspaper interview and I could see the pride in your eyes. And the day the man and his child from Jehovah's Witnesses came to the door, I looked the man in the eye and you, Andy, looked his child in the eye as I told them that their church had a damaging and unacceptable attitude toward gay people and I would not discuss it with them until they and their church had taken on the responsibility for better educating themselves in this area. You, Andy, saw the confusion in their eyes, the unsureness, and you said you felt sorry for them. I was heartened by your compassion and I was heartened by the look of sureness in your own eyes.

One of the parts of both of you that I value deeply is your sensitivity to other people and your capacity for compassion. We often have talks around the dinner table about public figures, neighbors, or friends at school. You are wonderfully perceptive in seeing how often negative behavior is related to a person's hidden pain or unhappiness. I know that the hours spent in those talks have helped to build your understanding and that I have tried so hard to facilitate this kind of understanding because I knew it would help you to understand gay people and the people who strike out at them.

Perhaps the most difficult person for us to understand together this year was Anita Bryant. At first you were thrown off balance, bewildered that a seemingly nice woman would want to strip the rights of citizenship from people like the many gay people you know personally. It would have been easy to see her as insane or a villain. But we had to go deeper than that. We had to work our way toward an understanding of how the world keeps changing, with social change in reaction to social change. We had to see how the social change had been accelerating in the past few decades and how people are now more easily frightened than ever. It was more difficult, but better growth, to understand her as the willing pawn of the forces in our society that stand to profit from some groups of people being kept down and relatively powerless. It made her actions no less evil but more understandable. It made her negative drama something from which we could learn.

There will be more of it coming along here in California this year and you are already talking about it. You can see already what too many voting adults cannot see, that the issue is not simply whether gay people are as entitled as any other citizen to become credentialed teachers, but rather whether one group of citizens at a time can be stripped of their civil rights so that the group in power can become stronger. You already understand what a basic threat it is to the foundations of democracy. And you are helping to see to it that these issues are discussed in your classrooms. I wonder if this could have happened if I were not gay. I want to believe and I do believe that my gay identity has forced all of us to stretch and put more effort into discussion and understanding so that we would not knuckle under in unnecessary shame. It has made me terribly proud of both of you and proud of myself.

I was really touched when I returned from San Francisco's gay parade this year, full of the enormity of it, touched by the quarter of a million visible gay people, moved beyond words by the flowers carried by individual marchers that became the gigantic memorial to a gay gardener who was murdered days earlier just because he was gay. What touched me when I told you all about it and we looked at pictures on TV and in news accounts together was your feeling of having been left out and your strong demand that you be included in the parade next year. I have never taken you because it felt like my cause, not yours, and because I still carry some presumed parental commandments in my mind that say I should not involve you in such matters when we have no idea yet whether you will grow up to be gay or not. Your sureness of wanting to be there, marching in the gay fathers' group and the feeling of hurt that you had been left out, made me pay more attention to your rights as people who happen to be children still. You will certainly be invited next year.

I stopped typing just now and looked around the room to gather my thoughts. I was thinking about how you are moving into adolescence now, Vicki, and how much effort both of us are devoting to building our individuality gracefully. You must follow your path and I must follow mine and we must keep alive the love and mutual caring that makes us so eager to follow one another's progress along those paths. And you are on the verge of the same process, Andy. I wonder if we would be so mutually respectful of the need for that individuality if I were not gay and we had not had to come to terms with that factor of "being different" all these years. I think not.

But what caught my eye as I thought this, is the books that you have out of the library now. One is about Martin Luther King, Jr., one about Annie Sullivan, and one about Helen Keller. What sort of youngster is it that takes these books out of the library and reads them along with the Hardy boys and Teen Miss, I thought? The answer is that these are the kind of young people I want to have in my life always. Full of life and searching you are, keeping up with what is popular among your schoolmates and thoughtful enough to want to learn about people who have been different.

If I have learned anything, it is that I cannot predict the future. You know that my lover and I have had serious talks about sharing a home. You know we would like to do that. You know that both he and I are concerned about how it would influence your lives and the lives of his children. We know our living together would be another of those actions-speak-louder-than-words examples about taking charge of your own lives and following the path of love. It is mostly logistics that stop us now, since his children and their mother have a halftime home base fifty miles away from the halftime home base you two have with your mother. It may end up that commuting will be necessary, if annoying, and I have faith that if that happens we'll find ways to get something extra out of it. Maybe we'll all learn from the pros and cons of living in a bigger family. We'll just have to wait and see. But whatever comes, I now know we'll do it together and we'll learn from it.

There is a gay fathers' group in San Francisco that meets

periodically and some of the meetings are potluck dinners with fathers and their children. We'll have to try one of those one day soon. It's another adventure, another membership open to us because I am gay and because you are glad to have a gay father. I see so many of those opportunities opening up for us in the future.

That's the gift we have given to one another. You made it necessary and possible for me to be openly and proudly gay. My being openly and proudly gay made it necessary and possible for you to learn early the benefits of exercising your unique individuality rather than hiding it in mock conformity. It has seemed hard sometimes but today it seems lucky all around. It makes me feel sad for those parents who try to force their children into a mold so that they will look like "respectable" citizens. They never will know what wonderful individuals they could have enjoyed for a lifetime within their own family.

So that's it. Maybe I should write you a letter like this every few years. It certainly does help me to see clearly how lucky I am to be a gay father.

* * * * *

And now more time has passed since that second public letter. We made the move to a big house in the city, my lover and I, his children and mine. It is a good home that houses quiet cozy times when two or three of us will sit together and talk or read and listen to music or watch the winter rain. Sometimes it is merry and colorful chaos when several people have friends staying for dinner or overnight. It is a home that contains a lot of hugs and laughter that far outweigh the moments of anger or tension.

We are in our second year of living in our home on the edge of the gay ghetto and it has been interesting to watch Andy and Vicki react to it. Sometimes I am uncomfortable when we are surrounded by costumed clones on the street and I fret about stereotypes being reinforced. But the two of them seem to be able to see the costumes as such without any prompting from me. We were sitting in the car, getting gasoline, when a man in full leather drag and dark sunglasses walked by. I thought it a menacing costume and winced inwardly. They commented to one another that he looked just like one of the singers from the Village People. I asked who the Village People were and learned of the singing group that had been riding high on a nationally popular song about the YMCA that had lots of gay innuendo in the lyrics. Two days later they delightedly pulled me in to watch as the group performed that very number on a network TV show. I sat there saying, "I don't believe this" while they knowingly chuckled with amusement. There on the screen were a group in a variety of gay costumes, singing suggestive lyrics with suggestive movements and all of America was watching and apparently enjoying it. I told Vicki and Andy that I was having culture shock similar to that which might have been experienced by a recently-freed slave transported forward in time to watch a middle-class black situation comedy on TV. They understood that, but continued to be highly amused because they had been able to bring their supposedly knowledgeable Dad up to date on something having to do with gay life.

From the beginning it has been comfortable for me to have them walk the city streets in the gay part of the city because I know they are more safe there than on most streets. I wondered how comfortable it would be for them, and soon found out. Vicki's class was gathering prizes for a raffle that would earn money for a class trip. She decided to ask merchants in the gay neighborhood to contribute. I forewarned her that they might be disinclined because the school was many miles away in another community and it would not be particularly useful advertising for them. She decided she would try, and to my surprise and pleasure she was able to bring in more prizes than any other single youngster in her class, all contributed by amiable merchants of our gay neighborhood. I need hardly say we were both quite proud when the prizes were listed with the telltale addresses and names such as "The All-American Boy" and "Out of the Closet."

Within walking distance of our house is the Castro Theatre, a wonderfully restored movie palace that has a live organist and is devoted to old and new films of particular interest to gay audiences. My lover and I went one evening with his youngest son and Andy to see *You Can't Take It With You.* Andy delights in all sorts of theatre but he particularly liked the enthusiastic audience that applauded not only the organist, but also the names of the producer, director, and actors as they came on the screen—and, for that matter, applauded good lines of dialogue. When the lights came on at the end, he looked around at the packed house and said, "It's a lot more fun coming to the movies here. People really know how to enjoy them."

Both Vicki and Andy have commented on how our gay neighborhood is like living in a small town within a big city. Very often we meet people we know on the street, in the grocery store, or in a restaurant. I think they appreciate not being put aside in the conversation or spoken to with condescension at such times. I have seen youngsters overlooked by adults in suburbia because children are more commonplace there and the adults seem to have a pressing need to talk to one another about adult matters. But when we meet gay friends in our neighborhood, they are as interested in meeting Vicki and Andy as they are in meeting me, and want to catch up with all three of us on what is happening in our lives, just as we want to catch up on theirs. I like the fact that children are treated as people rather than subadults.

My communication with my children continues, in person and in letters. It has been heartening to have their support and the support of others who love me in learning what I *can* be as a parent. Perhaps we would do well to shift the focus in that direction for all parents, gay and non-gay. What they cannot do as parents can be done by other willing and capable parent surrogates. But let us take on the adult responsibility, as parents, of fully investigating what we *can* do as parents *because* we are unique and different in some way. And let the adult community support the efforts of parents to use personal, individual differences to advantage in parenting. Some parents can't—but not because they are gay.

7

Sex, Sex, Sex

A standup comedian tells of a presumed conversation between Sophie Tucker and Sid. Sid is bragging about being eighty and having acquired a twenty-year-old girlfriend. Sophie answers that she is going to get a twenty-year-old boyfriend, reminding Sid that eighty goes into twenty a lot less than twenty goes into eighty. The audience howls with laughter.

In the film *Shampoo*, Julie Christie looks wide-eyed at the prosperous gentleman who tells her she can have anything she wants and describes the part of Warren Beatty's body that most interests her at the moment as she decorously descends beneath the tablecloth. Everyone, including me, nearly falls from the movie seats with laughter.

The same rules of humor work when the topic is sex as when the topic is something other than sex. But have you noticed how often the topic *is* sex? We are like a population obsessed. People are for it or against it, trying to score or trying to abstain, making rulings about how much of it is suitable for movies, television, children, even whether it is our con-

stitutional right to be exposed to it or protected from it. Every
ad agency and magazine rack in the Western world spills its
overflow of sexual stimulation. It sells tobacco and can be
cause for a diplomat to resign. It is almost impossible to get
through a day without having discussed sex in some way at
least once.

The wisdom of the ancients has repeatedly cautioned us to
remember that "less is more." The seldom-stated corollary is
that "more is less." Throughout my lifetime and for many
decades before, a lot of attention has been paid to sex in our
part of the world, whether in the name of indulgence or prohibition. We had no choice, therefore, but to be born into a
world where *more* has been made of the biological fact of
sex, thereby giving us *less* in human satisfaction.

How can we ever get it back to being a simple biological
fact of human life? The world is well-populated, so there are
plenty of other beings with whom sex could be possible. It
need not be treated as feast or famine. We could arrange our
world so that we had sex when the biological urge was present and went about our other concerns and occupations the
rest of the time. Once in a while it could be special—an un-
planned banquet or a planned gourmet experience, as opposed to the routine meeting of need.

One of our problems, of course, is that human history has
dictated that human sexuality be intertwined with other human needs such as power, love, trust and security. But we
live in an immensely creative age. Perhaps we could come to
view sex as simply sex, which becomes complex only when a
variable like power, love, trust or security is added to it in a
particular interaction. Perhaps we could begin to stop giving
sex the magical power to devour so much of our time and
energy. Perhaps we could make it *less* and thereby have it
render *more* human satisfaction. Easier said than done—but
we have had to cope with other major changes of perspective.
(They said that humans could never fly, and it once was
"fact" that the earth was flat.) We could learn.

One way that gay people are disadvantaged is that long

ago people in the Judeo-Christian world began to think of us as homosexuals—that is HOMOsexuals or homoSEXUALS, take your pick. Either way, what set us apart from the rest of the population was sexual behavior. The line was drawn right then and there. Nice people did not cross that sexual line (and if they did, they stopped being nice people). Of course gay people are as caught up in the sexual preoccupation as the rest of the population, which is enough of a disadvantage, but we have also been taught to view ourselves as people whose whole lives revolve around our "strange" sexual appetite. Obediently we tend to think of ourselves as sex-obsessed creatures whose obsession is not even of the approved variety. That can contribute to complications in human relationships when you put two or more such people together—and that is what happens since gay people, by definition, do not have sex with straight people.

It contributes to the booming business of gay bars. They are often the most obvious place to meet other gay people. Since we have been taught that all gay people are interested first and foremost in sex, we enter these meeting halls with sexual attractiveness (ours and theirs) in the forefront of our minds, insecurity at full pitch, fear of failure and desperation lurking in the corners. One is fearful of going up to another person and saying, "Hi, how are you?" He (or she) might think that means I am sexually interested in him. He might reject me because he is not sexually interested in me. He might talk to me only because he *is* sexually interested in me. Whatever is going on, the suspicion is that it is some sort of coded sexual bargaining unless you happen to know the person already. It cannot just be that you said, "Hi, how are you?" because the other person was there and you felt cheerful and friendly. What a shame. It makes it hard to meet people. Bar owners increase this anxiety by playing music so loud it is hard to hear voices. If you heard a civilized reply in normal tones you might be reassured, become less anxious, and order less alcohol.

Some sturdy souls overcome all odds in places like gay bars

and straight singles' bars and manage to meet real people. Most people end the evening having scored or not scored and are back soon, hoping for a better score.

And how about the way it affects established relationships? At least gay people are off to a slight advantage because they have had to deal outright with sexual issues. Non-gay people too often go into supposedly secure marriages with the assumption of death-do-us-part monogamy and find to their considerable discomfort that one or both partners gets sexually involved with a person who has nothing to do with the marriage. But even gay people have their troubles. Lover A finds that beloved partner, Lover B, has eyes for Candidate C. It may be that B and C have even shared an embrace, a kiss, or an orgasm. Lover A must go back to the assumed or stated contract and see if it has been violated. Whether or not it has been violated, Lover A must search feelings honestly to see if there is jealousy, envy, hostility, threat, or relief. Lover A must then decide whether to communicate the discovered feelings to Lover B and, if so, how. Should it be a civilized discussion or is it time to slash C's tires?

It is very complicated. The only thing one can count on is that any sexual contract or agreement between lovers must be revised regularly since the needs of each partner will continue to change. It is a rare couple that makes it through a whole lifetime of satisfying monogamy, or any other set arrangement. Given our strange training about sex, it is no surprise that most often the discomfort comes when one partner wants to be free to explore while feeling that the other partner should stay safely at home. Even if we are able to demystify sex, this imbalance is likely to cause trouble, since few mates like the idea of being left at home when their partner is off for a treat.

Sexual attitudes and acceptable behavior must be clarified periodically. I will probably have some different ideas about sex by the next time I dare to write on the subject; my understanding keeps changing, along with my personal needs and experiences, based on my dogged determination to see through the bramble that has grown up around this simple phenomenon. But I have decided on *my* current strategy, or how I will behave sexually with other people. My lover and I sometimes have periods of monogamy (security-building time—a safety zone) between periods of remembered appetite. We also currently use an "approved list" where feasible; that is, each of us has so far always been willing to cease sexual contact or not initiate it with another person if our lover vetoes that person. Other potential sex partners are on the approved list. The veto can be based on insecurity or a judgment that the prospect is unworthy—the reason does not matter. If a time were to come when it did not feel easy to agree to no sexual contact with a particular person, the whole matter would have to be reexamined. But so far, as I say, that has not happened.

But that is all background for my newly hatched sexual behavior program. What I dislike most is the hunt, both hunting and being hunted. The drama and choreography are interesting, but I resent the time and energy that goes into it and the predictable damage to honesty that accompanies such games as seduction. I also resent the guessing. Like most people, I am secretly shy when it comes to making my sexual desires known to other people, particularly strangers. Also, like others, I can bear rejection but it does not feel good, and I tend to avoid it when it seems possible. It is scary and sometimes humiliating to go around asking other people if they are sexually available to me.

I got to thinking it would be so nice if people would just let me know when they are sexually available to me and then I could respond to those with whom the feeling is mutual, if the time and place were ever right. If such a paradise existed, I would not always have sex with the people with whom I shared a mutual sexual availability, time and other considerations being what they are, but it sure would cheer up my world and theirs just to know how we felt about each other.

Then I thought about the advice I so often give to people who are searching for a lover. It sounds slightly mystical, but

it works. I tell them that when they have made themselves into the person whom they seek in a lover, the lover will appear. It works because, in the process of self-change, expecta-
tions become much more reasonable; the search for unat-
tainable perfection stops and is replaced with recognition of
worthwhile qualities in others. Also, you change yourself in
attractive ways.

Well, I thought, maybe that would work with sex. Since I
wish that everyone else would tell me of their sexual availability when it is true, with no expectation, demand or request for response from me in return, perhaps *that* is the person I ought to become. If I begin to behave that way with
other people, more of them will undoubtedly feel free to behave that way with me. Of course, I will use caution in making such announcements to total strangers. Some people still
take such a compliment as an insult.

It will be difficult to get over the shy hurdles and the fear of
rejection, but I can try. Change is never easy. It can take a
long time to become the lover (or sexual partner) for whom
you search. One thing is sure to happen—my attention will
be refocused from concern about whether a person is interested in me to a soul-searching answer to the question of
whether I am truly available to that other person (and why).

Since I am forty-eight years old and aging, I have more
than an academic interest in changes in sexual attitudes and
behavior that reputedly go hand-in-hand with aging. (Funny,
how the word *aging* is reserved for middle age and over when
we are aware that ten-year-olds and seventeen-year-olds are
also aging.)

Changes in sexual appetite, pressure, behavior and attitudes continue throughout a human lifetime, but like every
thing else human, these changes do not follow a neat, predictable pattern. One fairly predictable thing is the terrible
tyranny that sex exerts in late adolescent years for males and
in the fourth decade of life for women decreases with time.
Sex becomes more a part of life rather than the reason for life.
But, of course, there are individual exceptions to even that

simple rule—individuals who are totally ruled by sexual needs at other periods in their lifetime or throughout their entire lifetime. Another general rule seems to be that the more you use it, the more usable it is. True, like riding a bicycle, you never forget once you learn, but without regular practice the agility and delight may lessen. Also, older people generally report less involvement in sexual athletics and greater appreciation of the depth and aesthetics of sexual experience.

So much for generalizations. I notice in my work with groups that people are astonished when they find the myth of the age barrier exploded. Some younger people are surprised to find that they enjoy and can be aroused in touching older people. Some younger people come out of yet another closet by admitting that they have always been attracted to more mature people but thought that meant there was something wrong with them and that they should stick to their age mates. Some older people find that they can enjoy and be aroused by contact with younger people when they had spent years repressing such awareness because it seemed undignified (nobody wants to be called a dirty old man or woman). It is amazing how many barriers we have invented to keep people in categories. Age is only one, though it is probably one of the most common and universal.

A young man came skipping (literally) into my office a few months ago for his weekly appointment. He beamed at me and said, "I'm in love! I have known him for ten years and considered him a friend and mentor. Last night he came to my apartment for dinner. We were sitting by the fire reminiscing and we laughed about the times I had gone to outlandish extremes to avoid body contact with him for fear that he might want to seduce me. I realized all of a sudden that the whole thing had been my trip. I had always been afraid he'd see me as a twinkie and discount or even discard me. I looked at him and realized that his body has always been very attractive to me. I seduced him right then and there! He put up a fight but I'm younger and stronger so I won. We had a wonderful breakfast this morning. It feels like somebody has turned on the sun in the sky. His stomach isn't flat but neither is his mind. Wherever this goes, I'm awake now, and our love has another dimension."

Well said. Another piece of oppressive training laid to rest by one individual. I can also recall a similar event viewed by an older partner. A dignified judge sat in my office looking rather stunned. He had hired a young man to be his houseboy while he lived in Europe for six months. The young man cooked, cleaned, and was of great help in other ways, since he was trilingual and could sometimes serve as secretary-interpreter. The judge arranged to bring him back to this country when the six months was up. "I have only recently begun to realize what has happened. It became more and more pleasant to spend time with him. After that first year or so we managed to find ourselves in the same bed now and again and then sex became quite nice. Just last week, I thought of calling off the salary and household fund arrangement and simply opening a joint account. You know, he makes money tutoring. I now think it might be wiser to keep the old financial arrangement because it helps with independence—you know the sort of thing women are into now. But we sleep in the same bed every night. He is devoted to my well-being and I to his. He is not an employee. We entertain together, travel together, dream together, and share our most intimate secrets with one another. We have been with one another for eight years now. I think we're lovers! And here I've been moaning about wondering why I couldn't find love in the same way my friends have. I've found it my way, and I wouldn't trade." The fact that there was twenty years difference in their ages had blinded him to all of the other evidence.

This raises the question of sex and money or, more precisely, the question of sex *for* money. Prostitution is reputedly the oldest profession. We do not seem to mind paying money for almost any other kind of service imaginable. While prostitution today is often a matter of exploitation and hostility in disguise, it need not be. There have been times when temple prostitutes were a part of the way one saved one's soul. It does seem silly that we continue to cluck our tongues about a phenomenon that has shown such staying power over the centuries rather than using our creative intelligence to remedy its lacks and present ills. Other countries in contemporary times have demonstrated that the venereal disease threat to the community can be significantly lessened by having prostitutes learn to take precautions for their own sake as well as the sake of their customers. Like other professionals who rent their time and skills to the public, prostitutes could be brought under legislative control that would help to insure against disease (by requiring regular medical examinations to retain a license) or robbery (the usual procedure for bonding).

Prostitution could then be upgraded and become useful to the community in a number of ways. It need not be a demeaning experience for the professional who offers more than body rental for the customer who is in need. Earlier I expressed the hope that we can work toward a simpler view of sex as one variable that all too easily can become intertwined with other variables such as power, love, security and trust. We could have a large corps of professional sexual companions who were reasonably inexpensive for the short time their services might be required. The analogy would be the fast-food chains now serving us. They are fast, simple and inexpensive. They do not offer the best in nutrition and certainly they do not offer a dining experience that is memorable, but they efficiently eliminate hunger. Professional sexual companions could do the same with as much dignity.

If this were a regular and easily available service there is no doubt that many people would make use of it, particularly if it were legally and medically safe and went beyond inhuman mechanical acts. It would provide a base from which a person could learn to distinguish simple biological hunger for sex from more complex needs such as the need for sex mixed with genuine affection. On some occasions it might be far simpler if sexual need were satisfied by an efficient profes-

sional while affection is found elsewhere. Of course, there
would be other times when much more elaborate sexual experience would be necessary to meet one's needs.

I would also make a plea for the training of another sort of
sexual professional—the sexual counselor. I do not mean a
person who simply has sex with you. I am suggesting a more
advanced professional who would require more extensive
training in medical disorders, psychological malfunctions,
counseling techniques, and the complex factors involved in
rehabilitation. If we can ever be rid of our Victorian pru-
dishness and duplicity in matters of sex, it will be clear how
badly needed such professionals are and how highly esteemed
they should be for the service they might render humanity. It
is a long way down the road, but needed. Perhaps someone
will open a training center in a state that now legalizes prostitution.

Back to the issue of the categories that divide us sexually
and therefore divide us as a community of human beings.
Age is not the only one. What of sex for the disabled, or the
phobic boundaries of race, color, weight, and social class? I
have met hundreds, maybe thousands, of gay people who are
ahead of most of the rest of the population in recognizing
their limitations. Since the gay world produces more of the
pluralistic intermingling that was originally intended for this
nation as a whole, most gay people occasionally meet and
become fond of someone who is sexually repugnant to them
because of prejudicial training or inexperience with a person
of that age, race, color, nationality, weight, or physical disability. They want to express the affection in bodily contact
but find it difficult. That is where the average gay person is
ahead. He or she *want* to and knows it is his or her own limitations that stop it from happening. The average non-gay
person congratulates himself or herself for the inhibition, not
realizing it is an inhibition, but seeing it as a natural lack of
desire for someone with whom you are not officially mated
(forgetting the moment of transient lust only hours earlier for
some person of just the right age, race, color, nationality,

shape and physical ability to whom they are equally un-
mated and to whom they may well have never been intro-
duced).

My experience, and that of many of my friends and clients,
has been that massage is the gentle intermediary. If you feel a
real fondness for someone and want to express it in bodily
contact but are inhibited because of your own limitations,
you can always suggest a neck rub, a back rub, a foot massage, or even a full body massage (if you feel ready for that).
From the physical contact both people can sense whether
they mutually want to express their feelings with greater
amounts of physical contact that may or may not become
sexual.

I am using *sexual* in the too-limited sense of orgasm-ori-
ented activity. The word is often used in that limited way. It
is too bad because it limits our understanding of sex. Sex can
be a glance, a touch, a whisper, a stroke, or intercourse. A
severely disabled gay man I once met told me that he could
experience a thrill that was the equivalent of an orgasm from
the right man touching the back of his neck. His neck became
more private as it became more erotic and not everyone was
permitted to touch him there.

A gay man in his eighties told me that he enjoys sexual intercourse as much as ever, but there are now so many other
things he wants to do that he no longer has as much time for
it as he did in his twenties. He has limited it to his lover and
one old friend. Then with a twinkle in his eye had said he
would have to admit there *was* a third person. A masseur
who gave him a full body massage every week. "A young
fella, but he's got a sense of humor, you know, and hands that
were kissed by God. I almost always have an orgasm some-
time or other while he's working on me but I don't pay much
attention, just let myself go. It's a joke between us. Never
know if it'll happen while he's rubbing my toes or my nose."

He made me think that when I am older I would probably
want to be in some sort of protected community of gays
where there was physical and medical help at hand as

needed, but where one could live in beauty, peace, and privacy also. If I find or create such a place by the time I am in need of it, I will make sure they have some young energetic gays with a sense of humor and "hands kissed by God" who enjoy giving massages. They could be paid staff members of the residential community or caring volunteers. It would be a good way for some smart young people to build a bridge to their own old age so that they could enjoy life without so much fear of the future.

And let us not forget that sex is communication. A bothersome phenomenon that I see repeatedly is a couple who have painfully parted because they discovered the relationship was damaging both of them, yet they are pulled back together periodically by the magnetism of sex. The words say "go away," the sexual behavior says "stay here." Sooner or later they have to learn to say with words and body, "I do still care about you a lot but we cannot be together at this point in our lives."

Sex can communicate anything at any period of life. I have worked with three different sets of lovers in which one of the partners had a terminal illness. All of them said they wished they had learned to listen to the subtle communication of sex long before. And all of them were glad to have learned to listen in time to hear the acceptance of death and the bittersweet love message spoken sexually in a silent goodbye.

Sophie Tucker and her legend notwithstanding, eighty and twenty are more than numbers, and sex is a lot more than "going into."

8

Easy Does It

The little town where I grew up on the Atlantic Coast might have been more romantic and interesting if it had been a fishing village, though I sometimes look at travel posters of those picturesque little fishing hamlets and wonder how it is to live there rather than to visit them. Today you could drive to New York City from my town in an hour and half, but it took about three hours then and the big city might as well have been on the other side of the planet.

I always thought of my town, and still do, as a place where people were unnecessarily mean to one another. It was evident to me as child, but the sociological reasons were not. The Great Depression was upon us then, but since I had been born into it the world seemed normal to me. I know now that it created a lot of disappointment, bitterness, and fear.

The worst times were the winter months. In the summer people came from the cities to enjoy the white sandy beaches and the beautiful ocean. The natives were busy renting rooms, serving food, hustling souvenirs, and extracting money from them in every way imaginable. Concentrating on that distracted everyone from the habitual winter meanness. Also, since the weather was warm, good nourishing food grew easily in backyard gardens and vacant lots. Victory gardens became popular during World War II, but poor towns like mine had a head start on the idea. It seemed like magic to me that food grew free in the backyard. (I still feel the ghost of the excitement I used to feel when a brown paper bag from the grocery store is brought into the kitchen to be unpacked.)

In the wintertime the free food stopped, the "summer people" packed their suitcases and money to vanish like migrating birds, and it got too cold to fish unless you were a professional. As the weather got bad and people were idle once more, they turned their bad feelings on each other.

The whole town was poor but we were among the poorest. I am astonished that my family of seven was able to make it through those years. It took a lot of courage and creativity on the part of my parents and oldest siblings, a lot of willing work and making do from all of us. Sometimes there was no food at all. Other times there would be enough money for a banana and bread sandwich for each of us for school lunch. Many times my mother would make biscuits and, since we had no money for such extras as waxed paper, wrap them in clean dish towels that she had washed by hand, as she did all the laundry for a family of seven.

I remember taking the biscuits in dish towels and sitting at a green-topped wooden table far back in the corner of the school lunch room with the one sister and one brother who were still of elementary school age, the other children giggling and pointing at us. I remember carefully cutting a cereal box in the shape of my shoe sole and putting it inside the shoe, hoping it would keep out moisture and last until I got home from school. And I remember trying to hide the bottom of my shoe so that no one would laugh.

People were kind sometimes, of course, but even the kindness was often misguided and insensitive. I remember joyously bringing home from school the announcement of a free Thanksgiving dinner. I had not noticed that the invitation was given only to the poorest children in the class. My mother read the note and said she would have to go with me. I was even more pleased—two free meals! Not until the ladies in fancy dresses had finished the speeches, served the food, and I was taking my first mouthful did I notice that my mother was standing behind my chair. The mothers were not eating. They were not invited to eat, they were invited to witness the generosity of those ladies. The food suddenly did not taste very good. I was too timid to do anything but eat what was put before me, but I was ashamed. Throughout the meal I would sneak shy glances at my mother, who looked embarrassed and uneasy but would smile back at me in an attempt to reassure me.

All these years since, I have wondered how it might have been if someone had inspired that town to throw out its bigotry and prejudices. I wonder how it might have been if distrust had been replaced with cooperation. Times were poor, but working together we could have shared food and shelter, shared smiles instead of smirks, and gotten through those years with dignity and self-respect.

Everyone in that town was subjected to abnormal stress, first the poverty of the Depression and then the anxiety of World War II. The war finally filled pocketbooks but it also took lives, so guilt became the price of the better times. In addition, there was the nagging anxiety that we might be invaded by enemy troops since we lived on the coast. It hurts to remember it all but there is a point to it.

The point is the experience of stressful times. Some individuals had more stress than others because of fate, circumstance or individual makeup. Some were subject to additional stress within the community for being poor or for being different. At the bottom of it all was the phenomenon of people struggling with the bad feelings generated by stress and, all too often, trying to reduce personal stress by striking out at someone lower in the pecking order, someone who was different, thereby creating superstress for that person or group of people.

This is a phenomenon familiar to gay people. We are an

unfavored group. Our society is one generally characterized by plenty of stress. Unfavored groups must bear the normal amount of stress and, in addition, be subjected to the super-stress created when they are the target for people who are striking out, whether with ugly words on the street, discrimination in housing and employment, or a holy campaign to harass a group of "misfits." And more the horror if you are gay and unfavored in some other way—disabled, poor, black, ugly, or an immigrant.

Those gays who are able are learning constructive ways to rid themselves of some of the excess stress. They head for cities where they can become a part of a gay community. You can walk the streets of San Francisco and know that you are not alone because gay people are visible everywhere. Some gays have formed communes and gone to the country. Some have gone in twos or threes to find a small place safe from intrusion where they live on modest savings, retirement, or the work of their hands. Too many of us, of course, never make it. It is a race of sorts—a survival of the most able and fortunate, those who can make a run for it one way or another. If you are stuck in a place where you are isolated from other gays for too many years and are not gifted with superior inner strength, you may succumb to drink, drugs or suicide. We can still see the scars on some who have made it to the safety zone of gay communities.

We have learned some lessons and we have more to learn. We have learned to gain strength by joining with other gays. That produces more safety and reduces the stress. We have learned to strike out in legal and civilized ways at the individuals and groups who try to persecute us. This sense of strength and action also reduces some stress. Consciousness-raising groups, political groups, study groups, and pro-gay reading help us to discharge some of the poisonous beliefs about ourselves that most of us incorporated before we knew better. Feeling like a better person also reduces stress.

But there is more to learn. Many are learning it rapidly, but none too soon. We are learning to increase our tolerance for other members of our tribe. They may be different in political viewpoint or skin color, but we can do better than the people in the town where I grew up. We can learn not to laugh at difference as a way of hiding our own pain. We can learn to try to understand gay people who are different from our friends. We can learn to offer a helping hand to another gay person who is in pain even if he or she does not seem to be a person we would want for a friend. We can learn to cooperate and get through these dark years better than people of my town got through the first seventeen years of my life. There is no need for older gays to laugh at younger ones and dismiss them as "twinkies in butch drag" or for younger gays to laugh at older ones, calling them "nellie old aunties" or "Uncle Tomette." The younger gays may be trying to erase their own lingering suspicion that "faggots can't be real men" or "dykes can't be strong *and* be real women." The older gays are carrying scars from battles long ago and may have learned to camp it up and laugh too loud because they have seen too many tears. They may have had too many years of Girl Friday by day and persecution by night. There is no need for the bearded to laugh at the beaded, or the "fems" to laugh at "fags." We can do better.

But no matter what we do, no matter how cooperative we learn to be within our gay community, we can expect more stress than the average citizen. Many of us have taken a hard look at that and come up with plans to help us survive, starting with the basics. There *are* certain things one can do to survive stress.

The place to start is with your body. Take a look at the way you nourish it, exercise it, rest it, stimulate it, and abuse it. Having studied what you are doing with your body, you are certain to begin improving your care for the body that is you. But the trick is to take it easy. Remember, we have been taught that we are bad. There are shadows of that self-concept lurking in all of us. Even when trying to help yourself by taking better care of your body you may find that you whip yourself into a plan of action that does not feel good but "ought" to work. Since it does not feel good, another part of you will resist the plan while the first part of you continues whipping, and a civil war has begun within you. No side wins in a civil war. When the whip seems to be winning you are actually adding stress. When the resister seems to be winning you may experience yourself as a failure (again). You must find ways to help yourself that feel good and that harmonize with your experience and your temperament.

I took a long careful look at my body in a mirror and discovered that I did not like what I saw. While not obese, I was carrying more weight than I needed. Though I am not a youth, there were more lines of fatigue and strain in my face, particularly around the eyes, than ought to be there. My face seemed puffy too. Where to begin?

This self-help program has been going on some months. I am paying attention to the foods I like to eat and the ones I do not particularly care for. I am eating no more than usual of the ones I like and regularly eating less of the ones that do not tempt me. I have had to give myself permission not to clean my plate. I do not like waste and try to avoid it but the excess food will do less harm in the garbage than in my body.

Next comes drinking, which I know is contributing to the excess weight, the lines, and the puffiness. I like to drink. I have never seriously misused alcohol, but I have always been aware that I enjoy drinking with friends and have monitored it over the years. I am now aware of alcohol intake and asking myself if I really want each drink. Most dinners, two glasses of wine suit me better than three when I pay attention, but I am not making any rules. I did make a list of all the things I like to do in leisure time and picked out the ones, other than drinking, that I like to do with friends. I found that there were only a few, because a lot of the activities I enjoy are solitary—probably the result of having spent a lot of time alone during the growing-up years. I am on the lookout for other activities I may enjoy sharing with friends and look for chances to substitute the ones I already know I enjoy for those times when I would be tempted to drink. I am also trying weeks of no alcohol to break old habit patterns. The change can happen as slowly and naturally as it will. The easier it is, the more likely it is to last.

One idea that worked very successfully is this. Instead of the usual dinner party followed by hours of drinking and chatting, we invited friends for an afternoon of sun and massage, followed by a potluck dinner. We had time to talk first, then touch one another, then eat. It was one of my most satisfying social experiences. We all drank and ate less than usual, though the potluck spread was fabulous and the bodies around the table glowed with a different sort of high than that produced by alcohol.

Sleep and rest are important in body care. Fortunately I love sleep. All I had to do was pay attention to the times I was shortchanging myself and give myself permission to stop doing that by remembering it has a high priority. It feels fine.

Next comes exercise. Like everyone, I could work out a fabulous exercise program for myself and fail to follow it. I went back to my list of favored leisure activities and noted that I like to walk and swim. Hence permission granted to take more walks when I am in the mood, and to look for more opportunity to swim. I also have a moderate program of calisthenics that I have been doing for years and, while I do not particularly enjoy them, I feel better every day after I do them so I will continue. Recently, I joined one of those new gyms with lots of fancy equipment. As soon as they finished setting up a program with the proper amount of weights on each machine for me, I told them that for the time being I will use one less weight on each machine so that I can enjoy the exercise. And it is working!

I found to my horror that ways of stimulating my body and increasing awareness of it were poorly represented on my list. I like sex, getting massaged, and sitting in hot tubs (which is another way of visiting with friends that need not include alcohol). I will continue to get as much of each of those as possible and be on the lookout for other activities that may be stimulating and feel good.

As you can see, many of these activities, such as the hot tub, swimming, walking, and massage, and a few of my other favorites like sex, meditation, gardening, and needlepoint, are also ways of relieving body stress. There are others that have been useful and pleasing to me at other periods of my life and many others that are pleasing to other individuals.

All that is necessary is to look for activities that you enjoy and that also release tension. A good way to remind yourself of them is to create more leisure time. That usually means cutting back on some worthwhile activity like work. This has been the most difficult for me and I know it is for many gay people. I suspect that many of us overcompensate for those leftover feelings of badness by working hard to be the *best* whatever: best employee, best team member, best student, best parent, best lover, best salesperson, or best gay therapist.

When I looked at what I was doing, I found that my work as a therapist-counselor-consultant and my work as a writer are both extremely satisfying but I have been doing too much of both. I am changing that now, for the first time in my life, and what has facilitated the change is subtle. I am not forcing myself to cut down—that has never worked and never will work with me. I am giving myself permission to enjoy more leisure time *when it feels good*, and giving myself lots of assurance that it is all right to do so. To get the permission I had to see that I can be a better gay people-helper when I am rested and enjoying life. I also had to see that I will live longer to serve more gay people if I take more time off. With the writing I have had to give myself permission not to rush to meet self-imposed deadlines. The world will wait to read my words, and if I go more slowly maybe someone else will say the same things sooner and I can skip ahead to the next things I need to say. I am also giving myself permission to write in settings I enjoy, like sitting by the ocean. It may be less efficient but, again, I'll be around longer to write more.

Now when someone comes to the office wanting to work with me I feel all right saying I will probably be in the office between thirty-five and forty weeks of the year because I'll be

away with my writing six or seven weeks of the year and enjoying life otherwise the other weeks. Some people are
shocked, but after the initial shock comes the envy and the
urge to try a taste of it. Some people have work that does not
permit such a flexible schedule (and there were certainly lots
of years when mine did not) but ways can be found. A stolen
day or two, a surprise gift of an hour to oneself, and maybe
even a change of employment, are all possible. The important thing is not to work at not working but to take it easy, to
look for the easier way.

Last but not least is the importance of letting friends know
what you need. When you give information about yourself
and your needs to friends, it gives them the opportunity to
help in ways that they may enjoy quite a lot. A friend of mine
caught me at that hiding game recently. Knowing how much
I love massage, he observed my body tension at the end of a
day in which I had absorbed a lot of pain from clients. He
asked if I would like a back rub and I said "No, I know
you've had a hard day, too." His quick answer was, "I've
had a hard day in an office with papers and telephones, and
one of the reasons it was so hard was that there was no one
there whom I love and whose body I could touch with permission." My shirt was off in a flash, the lesson learned once
more.

In the days when it was first taught that it is more blessed
to give than to receive, people were accustomed to rubbing
one another's feet with scented oils. We all know feet hurt
after a long walk and friends hurt when under stress. But
they have to let us know how far they have traveled and
where it hurts before we have the permission to do what we
wish in helping them.

We are learning to help one another in ways that permit
everyone to gain. We are learning about stress and how to
reduce it. We are even learning not to *work* at reducing it.
We are learning to take it easy. Easy does it.

9

We Are Funny!

It is wonderful how you can meet another gay person through a mutual friend and within hours (sometimes minutes) of the introduction, you can be laughing together like old friends, sharing personal secrets it might take years of friendship to share with a non-gay friend. Not too many months ago I met a sprightly gentleman who, over a cocktail and some marinated mushrooms, talked of his recent move into a new apartment where storage was a problem. He lowered his voice and shifted his eyes in mock secrecy and said, "Of course, if it wasn't for all those steamer trunks with costumes of years past . . ." Wonderful. We were laughing at him and me and the world as created by old movies.

Then he said that on Halloween two years earlier he wanted to do a spoof on the heroines of 1940s movies. The lavish costumes, spangles, and headgear of that period lend themselves easily to satire. Humans were twisted into walking sticks of cotton candy, demeaned beyond sexual objectification.

He had nearly assembled his costume of chiffon, spangles,

jewels and heavy makeup when he remembered that he had once been an expert skater. He could be Betty Grable and Sonja Henie in one! There was no ice on the streets but someone he knew had a smashing pair of roller skates with high white boots.

An hour later he was skating merrily toward the street where the parade was traditionally held on Halloween. He had forgotten, however, that before reaching the parade he must cross a major thoroughfare with four traffic lanes. He had also forgotten that the preceding block was as steeply downhill as only San Francisco can be.

"What was a person to do?" he asked, wide-eyed. "It all happened so fast. I spotted the gas station at the corner and made a mental note that I could probably turn in there and get stopped somehow. I just hoisted up the chiffon and let the beads fly. By the time I was near the corner I must have been going sixty miles an hour—cars were honking and people were screaming. The light was red and I made a grab for the pole on the corner to swing myself around in the direction of the gas station. But, my dear! I was going so fast I went all the way around it in a flash, saw the light was green, made a smart leap from the curb and sailed across Van Ness Avenue to the thunderous applause of my audience. Then I had to stop to dry my panties."

His supervisor at the bank (non-gay) congratulated him the next day on his skill and daring. "I told him I was miffed that he hadn't noticed how *pretty* I was." That is San Francisco and that is gay humor.

We have learned to laugh at ourselves, partly as self-protection—alert to what about us might be laughed at by others—but also to convey the gentle message of tolerance that each of us is no better and no worse than we are. Our heritage is "Live and let live unless someone is being exploited or hurt." I once met an older gay woman of ample bosom. She announced that "My longevity is due to the judicious—and sometimes injudicious—intake of whiskey and buttermilk." She paused as if to clear her voice, with exquisite sense of timing, and continued "The whiskey has kept my head free from infection and . . . I presume we can all see where the buttermilk has went."

There is something about our humor that can cut through tiresome layers of pretense. It is a light way of presenting rock-hard truth. At the Halloween described earlier, one of my favorite characters was a "dirty old man." He slunk along the side of the street near the curb, close to the non-gays who had swarmed in from the suburbs for the show. His face was dirty, his old hat filthy, and he wore an ancient soiled overcoat several sizes too large. He strolled along the gutter, hands in the pockets of the overcoat, wearing a smile of demented bliss. Periodically he would open the overcoat, revealing that he wore nothing beneath but a condom.

That he wore only a condom in his shocking dirty naked-ness was a subtle sardonic note. The people on the sidewalk had come to be astounded and to laugh at the gays on their holiday. But his "statement" caught them by surprise because it went further than they thought he would dare go but not further than their fantasies had already gone. He literally presented himself as dirty, old, and a man, but also as a mirror. His silent performance cut through all the jokes ever told about dirty old men.

In the Mariposa film *Word Is Out*, subtitled "Stories of Some of Our Lives," there is a blonde ex-WAC, Pat Bond, who captures the heart of the audience. She is very funny and it is impossible to resist the pull of her ability to laugh at her-self and the rest of us. Her humor is incisive, as when she talks about how lesbians in the old days had to be "butch" or "fem" even when it did not quite work, like the "teensy tiny butch WAC who had teensy tiny little butch civilian clothes . . . a teensy tiny little pinstripe suit . . ." She would interrupt herself to roll with laughter. Her eyes sparkled with the humor but they could also reflect the pain in remember-ing how many of her friends had been hurt in a senseless witch-hunt.

That is part of our heritage that one senses and sees in gay humor. The pain is there with the laughter. I hope we do not lose it as we slowly integrate with the larger society. I notice less humor in these days of relative openness when in a gay bar or at a gay dinner party. Yet compared with non-gay functions I have attended over the years, I must admit that there is still much more humor in the gay settings. In a non-gay bar when everyone has had some time to drink one hears laughter, but it sometimes has a mean edge and it lacks depth.

Maybe we gays are watching our laughter more carefully these days. The witch-hunters are after us. We are accustomed to being an unpopular minority group and therefore always in some danger. But now the danger is greater and overt, with moves being made to legislate away our rights to housing, occupations and even choice of life partners. Blacks produced a lot of silly-funny comedians until they saw how dangerous it was to omit pride when confronting one's enemies. We are trying to see clearly when it is time to laugh and when it is time to be angry, lest we mock ourselves all the way to the segregation camps.

Perhaps what lends depth to our humor is our awareness of the simultaneous presence of comedy and tragedy. The Greeks of the Golden Age knew how closely the two were intertwined. One is never truly present without the other, its counterbalance there in the shadows. We are aware of it and willing to acknowledge it, which explains why so often there is a sobering pause in the middle of a funny story or a moment of laughter when telling of real-life tragedy.

Real humor may offer sudden perspective. I have a physician friend who is a respected specialist in a difficult area of medicine. He faces tragedy every day in his work. Not only is he a superior physician, but he has a wildly wonderful sense of humor. Sometimes when he does rounds, he takes a hand puppet with him. "It's all dressed up like a little doctor. I introduce him to the patients and ask if they mind if he asks a few questions and conducts the examination. Most of them love it! Of course, some of the ones who are still barely on this planet don't laugh—but they probably just think it's a smaller-than-usual medical student."

When he takes his puppet on rounds, he introduces the un-expected. People laugh and release some of their tension; it opens them emotionally to a new set of perceptions. The doctor is brought down to human size and can be seen as more boyish than majestic. It is a reminder that all things are possible—this doctor fooling around with a puppet. Maybe it is even possible to find new ways of viewing a recent and sudden disability. Maybe it is possible to face impending death with dignity and a sense of purpose. One has more options than those evident in the rigid rules of life and death prescribed by our society. This doctor has seen too much of life and death to care much about someone's opinion of his gay identity, so he is free to use it to draw on the depth of his gay humor.

I am quite fond of a gay woman who is a nurse. She looks a lot like Farrah Fawcett-Majors and she finds it fun to ride her very large motorcycle into the hospital staff parking lot, remove her helmet, then go upstairs and slip into the most "feminine-sexy" allowable nurse's uniform; she smiles sweetly into the scowling faces of old-timers on the staff who are keenly aware of her shift of role each day but dare not ask what it represents for fear that they will hear some real truth. She leaves them to deal with the churning battle of conflicting prejudices within while she goes on her way. "Not enjoying the best of both worlds as some people think," she says, "but enjoying *all* of *the* world—there's only one as far as I know."

Growing up or maturing as a gay person involves learning a suitable personal statement. Each of us learns a way to say, "I must do it my own way, thank you." We learn that we cannot afford to be dependent upon rules set out by others all the time. In a way, it can be seen as a brave statement of aloneness—facing up to an existential truth. It is a kindly flaunting of convention that hurts no one and reminds all gay people that what the world calls our madness is simply our truth.

I remember being in London one summer and going to a posh gay private club there. We dined upstairs and then went downstairs to a small disco. It was still early and there were perhaps a dozen people there. One man was on the dance floor, dancing. He danced alone, with himself, with the music, probably aware of the other gay people watching him. When the tape finished he left the floor to get a drink and only then did some others go onto the dance floor. It was as if he needed that time and space to make his statement of self. We all smiled because it looked odd—but we understood.

It would seem our humor does not desert us even in our darkest moments. I am thinking of two tales of near-suicide that I have been told. Obviously each person thought he was out of options and had no choice but to leave life. Both are now glad they stayed. One told of carefully driving out into the desert and meticulously hooking up a hose to the exhaust pipe. "Son of a bitch," he said, "it went just like everything else had been going for months. I had been told it was painless and odorless. They lie. It stinks! I realized I was going to be sick. I must have been fairly far gone but the prospect of that stench added to the smell of the carbon monoxide did not thrill me—nor did the prospect of the mess in the car. Tidy to the end! So I opened the car door to throw up and, of course, fell out and fainted."

The other man told of checking into a dignified hotel so that his ending would be decorous. He swallowed all of his pills and drank his flask of whiskey, got out of the suit and tie he had worn for the occasion, put on new pajamas and got into bed, "waiting to go quietly." The telephone rang. "It was the desk clerk. I had used a phony name so no one could find me but had given him the credit card with my real name on it. Could I please come to the front desk at once and straighten things out. So I dressed once more, including my necktie, gave him a personal check at the desk, and retired to my room once more. But the excitement must have pumped too much adrenaline or something. I woke up fourteen hours later with a hangover you would not believe."

Because most gay people have been burned by encounters with conformity, we tend to be upset and sometimes amusingly ambivalent when what seemed to be progress in life turns out to be a step towards conformity. A friend had spent many years of hard work preparing to become a bona fide professional. As he was nearing his final year he began to have doubts. Mulling over this turning point in life, he decided to have a little fun. He convinced a few friends who were as unsettled as he to dress up in drag and have an evening on the town. "I thought it would be good for our level of consciousness," he said, pretending wide-eyed innocence.

During the evening he got more tipsy than he had planned and more than the amount of alcohol imbibed should have made him, which happens sometimes when one is feeling anxious. In his altered state of consciousness, reasons for what he was doing were not clear. It just seemed that suddenly he was too tired to walk uphill to the street where he lived. Reasonable friends were dismissed and he took to the street, literally. His neatly trimmed beard and mustache had been pasted with tiny sequins to match the rest of his costume. He staggered unsteadily into the street on unaccustomed high heels, straightening the platinum wig and tugging to make the mesh stockings and gold lame bathing suit meet. A valiant attempt to coordinate the lighting of a cigarette with hitching a ride while managing the beaded bag unfortunately attracted a police car whose occupants were not amused.

Looking back on the thrills, horrors and subsequent amusement that evening provided, he was able to satisfy himself that he would not be pushed into some stuffy prescribed role as the professional he was about to become. He had made his statement—and he would hang on to the gold lame bathing suit in case it might be needed for future reminders.

That is a lot of what Charles Pearce, the female impersonator, is all about, I guess. He certainly draws audiences, gay and non-gay. He does a dazzling array of impersonations in one evening with impeccable timing and an inexhaustible reserve of humor. Perched on his artificial-flower-and-flashing-Christmas-tree-light-bedecked swing, pantomiming the half-song, half-scream of Jeanette MacDonald demanding that San Francisco open its Golden Gate, he is the Mad Hatter who reminds everyone not to get stuck in one character too long or they will miss their other selves. In one of his more elaborate gowns and carefully made-up face, he looks soberly out at the audience and says, "It takes balls to wear this dress." Balls, ovaries, whatever—it takes determination to be the many parts of yourself.

Gays, almost as often as blacks, are reputedly "the best dancers." There *is* something noticeable in the general populations though there is no doubt that there are individual gays and blacks who have enough trouble walking gracefully let alone dancing imaginatively. We may have rhythm but it is not very likely to be found in the genes since almost all gay people have had non-gay parents and grandparents. Perhaps it is because we have been told so often what good dancers we are. That must have some effect, the self-fulfilling prophecy.

Then again, it may be another manifestation of a sense of humor on a grand scale. You must have a sense of humor to get out there and move your body around in a manner that feels right and expressive and know that, no matter how silly you look to someone else, it not only will not matter in one hundred years, it does not matter now on the other side of the planet, and probably does not matter much to the people on the next block. It takes that sense of humor to see how foolish it is to presume there is a right way and a wrong way to dance. So let the parts of the body move as they will to the rhythms of the music and let the eyes fall where they may. Feelings get expressed through the movements. A lot of those feelings are sensuous because the act of dancing is sensuous and some of the other people on the dance floor are bound to offer some stimulus.

It is infectious. Gay discos are now being invaded in large number by non-gays who want to get that special spirit and feeling of sensuous freedom. They are looking for the *right* way to do it, which will kill the whole thing until the next gay disco opens. It is true, I guess, that once you see a dance floor full of people, women dancing to women, men to men, some alone or with some invisible god, the traditional mind set is broken and there is a feeling of "anything goes" as long as it is friendly.

I stopped in a gay disco in the suburbs that has become very popular and saw an enormous woman on the floor. She was about five and a half feet high and probably weighed in at three hundred pounds. She was doing a dance that was slow and innocent but somehow managed to exude sexuality. She was also making her own individual statement. Calmly aware that there was enough of her to go around, she was dancing with two women simultaneously, one on each side. We may laugh a lot but we do not kid ourselves.

Humor is used with great frequency in the weekend groups we conduct in San Francisco. It has often come under scrutiny. All I understood at the beginning was that I like humor and it got used in the group because it worked. In the decade that we have been doing these gay growth experiences, I have learned more about the humor. I now see how it is used to detoxify the atmosphere, to soften and generalize individual pain—as when someone has made a difficult admission to the group and there is a stunned, pensive silence. It is easy for the person to feel he has made himself an outcast. At this point one of the leaders will often say softly "Of course you realize you are the only person in this room who has ever felt that." People look startled and then their laughter convincingly says "You're not alone—me too."

Or the humor may be used in the group to cut quickly through to truth. One man staring at another says, "I am totally captivated by your gentleness and sensitivity." If apt, an alert leader may interject with "Yes, I've been following your gaze as it has rested on him. Your captivation is clear but I thought it was called tits-and-ass."

Sometimes I feel like the black woman schoolteacher in *Conrack* when Jon Voight scolded her for being so harsh with her students in the small, all-black school in the South. My humor in groups is sometimes designed to toughen someone while he is protected by the company of his own kind. I knew what the black teacher meant when she talked about the world outside being tough, and wanting to make sure her students survived. People can learn to take the laughs and see what is behind them, the better to have the last laugh.

I miss that weekend-group sharing of gay humor. After ten years, I have stopped leading the weekend groups myself, though they are continuing and changing in form as others now provide similar experiences for the gay community. When I wistfully commented on missing them to one of my colleagues (who sometimes led them with me in the past and continues to lead them now), he said, "We have faith in you, dear. You'll be making coming-out-of-retirement and cameo appearances regularly!" An appropriate dash of "dish," or gay humor.

Gay people on their way to maturity learn the necessity of questioning all the reference points (like *right* and *wrong*). Some of us get so practiced at it that we can do it quickly in a one-liner, incisively calling the question on an insufficiently challenged basic assumption. When done quickly, as in a one-liner, it causes a cosmic tickle that makes laughter irresistible. People unaccustomed to such a quick turnabout are sometimes made too anxious to laugh. It is one reason why much gay humor falls on deaf ears when non-gays are present. A non-gay may find such heresy frightening. We have already had a large dose of fright and take comfort in huddling together under the umbrella of humor.

Some years ago, I was walking down a street near the docks in New York City with an old friend. It was dusk. There were several leather-and-western gay bars nearby. We saw a biker park his motorcycle a block and a half ahead of us and begin walking toward us. He was done up in full leather drag from the studded black cap to the studded black boots. Just before he passed us, he missed his footing on the uneven sidewalk. My friend, who had new dentures as of that day and was not speaking too clearly yet, could not resist a *sotto voce*, "Watch the heels, honey," as we passed. The leather gentleman, without letting a fraction of a second pass and without looking in our direction, said, "Easy for you to say."

10

Every Man Should Own a Dress

During two of the last few years that I was married, there was quite a nice black dress hanging in my closet. It was not there because my wife had no room for it in her closet but because I had shopped for it, picked it out, and purchased it to wear myself. Admittedly, it hung in the farthest corner of my closet, but then I wore the other things more often. When my glance fell on it hanging there, I experienced a moment of shock followed by a fleeting shadow of shame. It took the starch out of my masculine sails and not infrequently it set off a train of stray thoughts and questions about my identity: "Who am I, anyway?"

The last months that the black dress hung in my closet, it began to take on a stature of its own. It was almost like a political statement and I wished that people would see it, but how do you casually invite guests to browse through your closet? It left my closet finally because it was given away and replaced, but that is a story in itself.

The political statement my black dress made in its final months began as a question that changed to another question and then evolved into a statement. The first question was: "I wonder if any other men in this family suburb have a dress in their closet?" I sort of knew the answer to that question even before it was asked. I had been a clinical psychologist in practice for enough years to know that there were plenty of men who owned dresses and loved to wear them. I also knew that half or more of the real transvestites were dyed-in-the-wool heterosexuals who got off on women's clothes as well as women's bodies, so by laws of chance there must be a couple of those men in my suburb.

The question that replaced the first question was, "What if every man in this town owned a dress?" That set off a variety of thoughts, fantasies, speculations and emotions that were sorted in the odd moments of many months. As a result of those months, the statement was born. "Every man *should* own a dress." It became perfectly clear it would make a better town, nation and world. Now let me backtrack and try to tell the major chapters of this story of change.

It seems to me that I had a sour reaction of distaste most of the years of my life when I heard "camp" names being used, men being called by women's names and women being called by men's names. Not surprisingly, the reaction was stronger when it was a man being called by a woman's name. Sometimes it was amusing or kinky to hear a woman being called by a man's name but then tomboys have always been more acceptable than sissies in our world—part of our devaluation of women.

As I got reacquainted with my estranged gay identity near the end of the fourth decade of my life I started spending more time with gay people, so exposure to camp names was more frequent (though I was relieved to find they were less in style than they had been in my teen years when I made an abortive entrance—more a peek—into the gay world). An unexpected "Listen, Mary . . ." in a deep baritone, when accompanied by hand on hip especially, could stand the hair of my neck on end—and I feared going into shock if the person dared to address those words to me.

When I started working professionally with gay people, individually and in groups, I whipped up an elaborate rationalization about how we had been trained to think of gay men as false women and gay women as false men and we must not continue to reinforce this sort of identity assassination and battering of self-respect with cross-gender names. Of course, the only reason people were willing to listen to my ravings was because they contained a germ of truth. It is wrong to think of ourselves as false anything, and to that extent it did reinforce the homophobic teaching of a sick society. But most of the preaching accomplished the primary mission of making me feel better and lessening the chance that I would be exposed to such unnerving language.

All during those early years when my consciousness was making its hard climb up, every time a camp name was used and I heard it, I was not only uncomfortable but something in the back of my mind tugged at my awareness. It reminded me of something else. But the something else, respectable as it was, stayed respectably compartmentalized in my head and the two did not meet for years. It happened one day when I was having a discussion with a Jungian friend and colleague. I did not even dare say my thought aloud at first! I would not want to hurt my friend's feelings or impugn the honor of the theorist whom he so respected. As my phobic fog cleared, it was obvious that the gay subculture had been comfortably handling the concept *anima* and *animus* for ages. Everyone was quite comfortable with the woman inside the man and the man inside the woman—everyone but me, so it seemed. It was later still that the professional thinking about multiple personalities and multiple facets of the well-integrated personality clicked into place and became useful also.

The newly dignified concept of the meaning of camp names enabled me to try out some of the language with a few close friends though I was still apt to blush if my defenses were not firmly in place. But like everything else, usage made me more comfortable with camp names—provided there were only gay people present. If a non-gay person was present I would be embarrassed. If a non-gay person I knew well was present, the embarrassment was profound and the blush returned. Old phobias die hard.

I do try to learn faster nowadays (my first grade teacher would be happy). Before my own comfort level was quite ready for it, I proposed the idea of a drag night in each of my ongoing weekly groups. I believe it was near Halloween so the idea of "dressing up" had a little more support from the general culture. Several people in each group were quite enthused and more were extremely reluctant, with protests ranging from "I could never find shoes in my size" to "You'll never get *me* in a dress." We spent enough weeks talking about it that Halloween came and went, thereby making the upcoming event even more anxiety-provoking. The discussion was good for everyone, including me. I began to see how deeply ingrained is the fear of loss of central identity and, for men, how related it is to the fear of loss of power. The drag night has now become a yearly event but, almost without fail, there is at least one man in each group who flatly refuses and comes to that group evening in his usual male drag.

My preparation for the first drag night seemed like a never-ending series of frightening or embarrassing events. First I borrowed things from women friends if there was some hope I might fit my six-foot frame into their garment. I put them all out on the bed one evening just after dinner and decided to get it over with by trying them on to see what would fit and what would not. My wife joined me to supervise, advise and giggle. My children were outside playing but came in to ask about something, found the show fascinating, and invited their friends in to watch also. I could not very well protest since I was pretending my consciousness was more raised than it actually was, so I performed my bizarre costume act before this unusual audience. Finally everyone, young and old, got behind it and offered serious suggestions about what looked good and what looked silly. But no matter what I did, I could not assemble an outfit that did anything but make me look like an uncomfortable male in borrowed drag.

But there was a man I had known for some years who had

been in the first gay group I did in New York City. He was now living nearby in California and had been "dressing up" and enjoying it for years. I explained my problem on the phone and he said "A big girl like you should know you can't get by on borrowed stuff. We'll go shopping on Saturday." I could not believe I was doing this, and pretending it was an everyday event besides. We were going to go shopping in the suburbs, starting in the fashionable thrift shops in the small town where I lived.

The first store got me off to a good start. We sailed in, to the astonishment of the two proper ladies who ran this charity turn-about store, and my friend headed straight for the racks, pointing imperiously over his shoulder to me and saying "Something in large for that one." I stood right there in that small shop trying on dresses, gowns, furs and jewels over my rugby shirt and jeans until it became obvious I had to go into the dressing room and remove the male clothes to see if I was getting a good fit. We went to many other stores that day, but returned to the first one to buy my precious black dress with hand-detailed work. It had been a hundred-and-fifty-dollar dress, never sold (probably because it was too large), and I got it for thirty-five dollars. It was smashing and looked elegant when worn with jet beads. The two ladies had become enthusiasts in the project after their initial shock wore off. One of them even called my office a month later to tell me that a fur had come in that she thought I would love. The answering service has never quite recovered. Strange world.

The second trauma of that never-to-be-forgotten shopping spree was finding a wig. We found ourselves in one of the most fashionable department stores. The woman clerk looked dazed at our entrance but I was getting used to that. My friend said "I think something in a bright blonde . . . ," and began industriously sorting the stock. The saleswoman stood immobilized.

"Is that a wig you're wearing?" he asked her with a friendly wink.

"No," she answered, face still a blank.

"Pity," he said.

He now had me in front of a dressing table mirror, jamming one wig after another onto my head. I am a person who has never worn hats and I did not like the feeling. "Sit still and try!" he commanded, attacking each wig with comb and brush. "We have to soften the contours of your face and cover the sideburns, dear."

Half an hour later we left with a wig, walking briskly to the makeup department, where a young saleswoman had been eavesdropping unself-consciously on our show. "Got something that can cover those wrinkles, dear?" he asked, again pointing in my direction.

She said the things they had were too expensive. "What are you guys doing, anyway?" she asked as we hurried off in the direction of jewelry.

My friend called back, "Putting him in drag, obviously."

"Oh! Far out!" she called. "Good luck."

By this time I was only half in shock and half enjoying it. The world was more flexible than I had assumed and we were obviously turning an otherwise drab working Saturday into a fun day for a number of people.

The next struggle came the evening the group was to meet. Getting the makeup on was a harrowing experience. I was willing to accept supervision and suggestions, but felt by then it was important that I do it myself. I had the usual mixed audience offering suggestions. I went to the dinner table in makeup and bathrobe so as not to soil my dress. What a bizarre evening. Every time one of my children would address me as "Daddy" it would be followed by a short giggle.

When all was assembled I wobbled out the door on high heels, with purse instead of briefcase, ears being pinched by earrings, a headache developing from the wig, cheers and good wishes following me. I started the engine of the car, checking the rearview mirror as usual before backing out of the drive. A woman looked back at me from my rearview mirror! I almost lost it then and there. I had been prepared for the transformation in the bathroom mirror but not for the woman who suddenly appeared in my place in the car. As I drove carefully to the office I fretted about the myriad misadventures that could happen, such as a flat tire or being stopped by the police for some reason. These things have actually happened to other people on subsequent drag nights and both they and the police survived, but I certainly was not ready for it that night.

That was about seven or eight years ago and I am still not totally comfortable with drag night. It represents one of the deepest self-probes I have ever attempted. Every year I hate it and every year I learn more. If you try to retain your usual mannerisms in such a radical change of costume, they immediately look and sound out of place. In order to find some degree of harmony and therefore comfort, it is necessary to let hidden facets of your personality produce new mannerisms. It is quite unnerving at first. What most men do is act out some caricature of a woman (usually not attractive) at first, but that caricature also does not fit and they find they must yield eventually to some "feminine" truth hidden within the self that fairly represents them and is in harmony with the costume. The drag costume itself becomes more and more important with repeated experiences, since it must fit you emotionally as well as physically.

Every point of reference seems to change. Authority must be presented differently or it is resented. Gestures of friendliness and attraction must alter lest they seem stilted or overstated. The look and meaning of age changes. You are forced to notice when you look in the mirror that there is a different person looking back at you than the one you usually see and you have different feelings about that person than you usually have about yourself. And the other men in the room are all undergoing as many changes and more, so that it is an entirely different group of people relating to one another in totally different ways. There is an underlying current of anxiety throughout the evening, waiting for the end when people can take off their costumes and reassure one another that the old self is still there. It reminds me of the time I was in the bathroom shaving with lots of lather on my face when my daughter was only months old. She toddled to the door and pushed it open, beaming up into what she anticipated would be her Daddy's face and burst into a scream of anguish because he had magically been transformed into this other creature. Even after quickly wiping away the foam with a towel, it took me many minutes to console and reassure her.

The first few years, I fumbled for a format for the drag evening. The usual group could not work since the dynamics of the group were entirely changed. I usually used some variation, having each person stand in the center or walk about while the rest of the group merrily projected what sort of woman they thought this was. The person would then respond, after having heard everyone, by telling the kind of woman he had tried to portray and giving honest feedback on which of the statements he had heard had an impact on him and represented something he sensed he needed to think about or explore further another time.

This year when we did drag night I asked each person to try to get in touch with some facet of his personality, using the concept of multiple personality presented in the *The Three Faces of Eve* and *Sybil* as exaggerated illustrations of the many facets we all have integrated into one personality. The instruction was to seek a true facet of self that could be expressed more easily in the form of a woman than in the form of a man. They were urged to shop for appropriate clothing for this person (taking along someone else from the group for moral support) and to try to stay in character as this person throughout the evening.

So much is learned! First come the superficial but important discoveries about how oppressed women have been by their clothing: restricting quick assertive movement, pinching here and there, rearranging the natural shape of the body, and covering the color tone and texture of the skin as if even this were unacceptable in its normal state. On the other hand, the new costume lets out parts of self usually held in check by customary male costume; movements tend to become more fluid, more softness appears, and there are surprising displays of spontaneity, intuition, bitchiness, tears, narcissism, flirtatiousness and easy compassion. It is so clear that these things are coming from within and have been held in check there for a long time.

At the Gay Pride Day parade in San Francisco this year, I picked up a wonderful idea from a gay psychiatrist who had discovered the utility of drag in one of my weekend groups. He is from another city and was here for the parade. We talked excitedly on the street corner like two cooking students exchanging recipes. This group had hit on exactly that idea for drag night—recipes! Each man came dressed as the woman within and brought a dish she would bring to a potluck dinner. They stayed in character all evening. One brawny man, usually clad in plaid flannel shirt and jeans, had been transformed in a chic, expensive, understated dress. He had also acquired a French name, slight accent and had prepared a paté with his own hands. Another usually too-tasteful gentleman turned up in Sears' best, chewing gum and cheerfully carrying a bucket he had picked up at Colonel Sanders. And they all dined together making suitable conversation in an unusual group! I tried it out at the next drag night and it was a wonderful evening of fun and learning.

These experiences with drag have led me and other group leaders to use an increasing amount of other old-fashioned camp jargon. In an all-male group, when break time is over, I will call out, "Okay, girls, let's get it together! Straighten the stockings later, we need to get on with it."

This has precipitated outraged remarks about low consciousness and lack of understanding about the principles of feminism. Misogyny has been charged more than once. But what happens is that it teases out the anxiety and reluctance that men have in showing "feminine" parts of self and the underlying fear of loss of power if they trade male identity for female identity. It is one thing to mouth words about how "people are people" and "sex roles are destructive" but most men, including enlightened feminists, would prefer to keep the male role and its traditional privilege as long as there are any roles being kept—and the roles will still be around for a while. They can handle the concept "walking a mile in my brother's shoes" but they are not quite ready to go a mile in their sister's dress.

With the help of some eager friends, I have been developing the major "female" facet of my personality, giving her permission and air to grow and I find that she is evolving. I was quite dubious about her when she made her appearance. She is a person who tends to tell the truth without editing, assuming other grownups can take care of themselves. She was named the day she walked into a friend's house to be shown a new desk of which he was quite proud, a handmade reproduction of an antique. She said "It is gorgeous, absolutely beautiful—totally nonfunctional of course—but beautiful!" "Bunni" received her name and a brief fictional history within the next hour. Our impression of her at the time was that she liked to wear comfortable, fashionable, expensive, designer-made pantsuits while sitting on the bar stool at the country club with martini in one hand and cigarette in the other, dispensing her droplets of truth and not caring much whether they were listened to or not. She also has a nostalgic fondness for springalator (no backs) shoes that she likes to flap as she sits crosslegged at the bar.

It was Bunni who went to the next drag night, in character for the evening. She found some of the talk untruthful and some boring and was sure she was tired about fifteen minutes before the evening was over so she picked up her purse, told everyone she was tired, and went home. Don't think that did not set off some reactions in the group. "Don would never behave like that!"

As close friends and I have gotten to know Bunni better we see there are many dimensions to her. Just two evenings ago a friend said, "I think she grew up quite lonely, plain, and probably poor. Her name was probably different then, maybe Laura, and Bunni was a nickname that came later when she met sophisticated people. That's what saves her from being a bitch. There's a natural depth and understanding that shows through even when she's letting the chips fall where they may."

I have gotten to like Bunni quite a bit and she and Don go out in public together more and more often. That is what it is all about, after all, salvaging parts of you that have been hidden and letting them come to life so that they can grow and integrate with the rest of you.

Had it not been for the permission that helped Bunni emerge, I am not sure I would have found her more mature sister—another facet or later stage of my anima that has been emerging in the past year. She is so much like the title character in May Sarton's novel *Mrs. Stevens Hears the Mermaids Singing* that her name may remain Mrs. Stevens. She is bringing much richness to my life by permitting appreciated facets of me to emerge. She is not often concerned about wardrobe so I am spared any extended shopping expeditions before she appears at a group drag night. She is much more relaxed than Bunni but they are related and Bunni still appears with truthful tongue when she feels the need.

The original black dress, by the way, I gave away at a weekend group to a man who was far too stuffy as a man. I hope it has hung in his closet, if not on his frame, and helped him to soften and appreciate the quite wonderful other side of himself.

11

Integrity, Dignity, and the Right to be a Fool

Dignity and the right to be a fool are the by-products, or symptoms, of integrity. When the self-core is strong, solid, and flexible, these two outer manifestations become visible to the world. Imogen Cunningham, the photographer who worked as an artist into her tenth decade of life, was a person who demonstrated these qualities. Perhaps they were forged when as a young woman she determined to be an artist, not an easy goal for a woman in those days. Like gay people, she had to learn who she was and continue to become that person. She could not afford to have the world define her. The "suitable" roles available would have prevented the integration of her parts. She is described as a strong-minded person serious in her work, sometimes taking risky leaps ahead, willing to clown, amused by the shock or surprise of those who watched her, interested deeply in other individual lives—a person who walked her path with grace. One indicator that she was genuine in her integrity was that her *way of being* captured attention in a manner that made you think. It was not slick, packaged or easily understood. She was "different," that is what made you think. "Why did she do that? Why didn't she do what a person ordinarily would do in such a situation?" The answer, of course, is that she was not ordinary. Her integrity made her individual and therefore odd. If you are going to try for integrity, you must risk being odd.

Wholeness and strength come with integrity. You build integrity by finding all of the pieces of yourself, owning them, respecting them, and then fitting them together as you would a three-dimensional puzzle. It means facing the parts of self that may at first seem unattractive and better kept out of sight. But if one piece of your personal puzzle is missing, the entire structure will be weakened.

Take a look at Jim. It is not his real name, of course, but he is real. He appeared in my office six months ago looking like the Tarzan of my childhood movies, except that he wore a business suit and tie. His voice was deep, sure and loud. His gym-developed muscles showed through the business suit when he moved. His broad white smile communicated charm, ease and ability to take over any situation. It was the lines around his eyes that gave him away. There were lines of pain and sadness. He was married, with children almost old enough to be on their own. He and his wife had a marriage that was the envy of all their friends. One problem: He had tried to commit suicide a half dozen times in his life and no one knew it. He could feel the despair coming again and he was afraid he might try again and succeed. And this time things were different. He had met a man. While he had experienced fleeting sexual encounters with men throughout his adult lifetime, they had been secret and he had punished himself for each experience with self-loathing and superhuman attempts to be an even better husband, father, executive, and valued member of the community. But this time it was different. He liked the man and had seen him more than once. He suspected the feeling was love and to his own horror found himself wanting to tell others about his new friend. More than ever before there was a reason to live. More than ever before there was a conflicting urge to punish himself with death.

We worked together for several months. Then he felt he was moving too fast and needed time out to take stock. During our time together, I could see his integrity and strength building. He found parts of himself that he had only glimpsed at times when he was drunk. He took pleasure in the sight and feel of his body. It was no longer a display of manly muscle to mislead other people. He learned that he needed to cry and feel tenderness in the arms of a man. He learned that it was safe to be a peer instead of a competitor with another man. He found his anger, which had been unacceptable to him when he was trying to have everyone like him. He found his greed and resentment connected with stored-up need for love with another man. And he found many other parts of himself revealed in dreams and defenseless lovemaking. Slowly the pieces fitted together. Suicide was no longer tempting. There was too much to live for. True, the present agonies and those that lay ahead were frightening. But fright and timidity were newly discovered parts of his self that had to be accommodated to make it whole and strong. He was looking ahead to the probable end of a marriage, the shattering of his reputation, and possible rejection by his children because of false values he had helped them to build when he was a pretend person, and to a career that was already ending. The last time we met he cried through half of the session. As he was leaving the office, he said, "It's odd. I know I don't see things clearly because this is a time of change. There was a time when if I had cried I would have thought myself a weakling. Now, it's *because* I am crying that I know I am going to make it. Without the tears I could have been broken. The tears make me strong. I can heal myself and let some other people help. I don't have to be strong on the outside and hollow inside."

But how is one to go about locating the parts of self and integrating them into a strong, whole self? It is difficult for older people who have become set in their ways. Their carefully assembled self-understanding must be questioned, which can be painful and frightening. It is also difficult for young people because it is hard to know whether parts of self are genu-

ine since they have not had the test of time. Testing presumed
parts of self in new situations is also painful and frightening.
The older person who has presented herself or himself to the
world as happy-go-lucky may meet hostility when making
needs known. The young person who believes he or she has
an uncompromising sense of justice may discover the rights
and wrongs, goods and bads, hard to sort when beloved
grandparents file for divorce and begin to make charges and
countercharges. And to make matters more complicated, the
self keeps changing. To be sure, it changes slowly in time. It
evolves without ever reaching an end. Some people mistake
rigidity for integrity. If there is not change with time, one has
not tapped the self-core but is slavishly following a set of
rules.

How to find the parts of self and examine them? There is no
one suggestion that works for everyone. Psychotherapy,
diary-keeping, talks with a best friend—all of these are very
helpful. A gay woman with whom I have consulted infrequently over the past half dozen years found a unique road
into her self. It started about a year after she gave birth to a
baby girl. She fretted about the values she was unconsciously
reinforcing in this newly arrived individual, anxious that her
daughter should develop as her own unique self and not be an
extension of her parent. This led to a fantasy bedtime story,
told more to herself than her daughter, about a wonderful
kitchen oven that got computerized and began to develop
feelings along with astonishing talents. The story had an additional chapter every night. The oven moved away from its
wall station and became a mobile kitchen helper and finally
had the run of the house as an odd but energetic member of
the family.

She came in for a talk a year after the story had been begun. "Somewhere along the line, I realized that this was a
substitute for pushing those values onto my kid. God bless the
oven. As the story grew and grew I found I was responsible
for choosing every right and wrong and its consequences for
my android. And it all had to be consistent—you know,
things couldn't contradict. Anyway, then I realized the

damned thing was me. The story had given me just enough distance so that I could examine me. I found some pretty ugly parts of me. With a few of them—like talking behind friends' backs so as 'not to hurt their feelings'—I just had to clean up my act and say it to their faces or not at all. I mean how can an oven hurt your feelings? I had to see I was protecting me and not them. Other parts, like finding I had a temper, I just had to accept as part of me. So an oven has a temper—big deal! As long as it doesn't get nasty and burn somebody. I found out I wasn't nasty that way. My mobilized oven househelper liked to let people know when it was hot and even open its door now and then to cool off, but it would never attack anyone."

The search for parts of self to be integrated is a process that happens over time; indeed, it is a process that takes a lifetime. New facets of self are constantly uncovered once you have developed an orientation of openness or receptivity that permits glimpses of self previously kept in the shadows. It helps if you remember that much of what you will discover is good news, once you get past the newness and rarely do you lose anything except those outgrown parts of self that have been carried along like dead weight out of habit.

Last night I was invited to dinner by two old friends and I was struck by the evolution of their separate lives and their shared life together. They live in a house in the country. They bought it about two years ago. It was a pleasant old farmhouse and they have been slowly changing it. First the old windows came out and were replaced by huge windows that brought the outdoors into the living room. The plaster walls were covered with wood to harmonize with the natural setting seen through the big windows. The changes have continued week by week. Visiting their home is a thrilling experience. It is like watching a painting being created. Sometimes there is a bold brushstroke like the windows and sometimes a perfect tiny detail—like a small lithograph which has been moved from room to room and how has found its rightful place in a guest room. It is in perfect harmony with the rest of the room.

This led me to the realization that their lives have been like that too. There has been the continuing process of locating parts of self and finding the right space for them. One of them was a staunch intellectual who has been a hungry consumer of books for the nine years I have known him. But his self-concept had locked him into the world of words, printed and spoken, with little room for the nonverbal mysteries of life. Since they joined and moved to their farmhouse, he has discovered a love of cooking. I can remember when he was truly impressed with someone who whipped up a quiche in a frozen pie shell. For dinner last night he prepared a salmon mousse with a sauce made from sea urchin roe that he had gathered that day, boiled new potatoes in their red skins, asparagus in a butter sauce, and a glazed strawberry pie for dessert. The table arrangement was a simple work of art and the quiet absorption in his face as he eased the sauce onto the mousse with a ladle conveyed satisfaction and peaceful enjoyment. He was not busy with words. He has found part of himself which he had not allowed himself to see when he was operating with a culturally defined male identity. The big step into a loving relationship with another man has begun opening doors that reveal other parts of him. He still goes through piles of books and is excited by ideas. New has been added without diminishing that which was genuine in the old.

His partner had been a confirmed city dweller who climbed steadily in his profession, played a grand piano, and busily dedicated himself to the city's pleasures after a two-year heterosexual marriage ended when he admitted to himself that he was gay. Last evening he proudly showed me the wiring he installed in the kitchen and the bookshelves he designed and built in the livingroom, touching them lovingly as he did so. After the beautiful dinner, he sat at the grand piano and played the second and third movements of Beethoven's *Pathetique*. He has lost nothing but has added another dimension. And together they talk about the swallows that have built a nest under the eaves and the continuously changing colors of the landscape. Together they have opened doors and found parts of self that are fitting with the already discovered parts. It was very moving, and a good reminder that the process of building integrity is not all pain.,

This is the gift that gay people have to offer others. Though the first admission of profound interest in people of the same gender is difficult and often painful, it can set one's foot on the path of integrity. It is as if the inner voice says, "If this is true of me, what else is also true?" Having faced something that seemed unthinkable to face, we are ready to face whatever else is true. And for non-gay people the process is sometimes strikingly similar—the mother who admits to herself that she was not cut out to be a parent or the career soldier who faces the inner reality that killing is wrong. We test our steps along the path of integrity with time and experiences. The mother may find her unfolding truth forces her to admit that parenting has limited but vital satisfaction for her and she can enlist the aid of others to help with good parenting. The soldier, after early retirement, may find deep satisfaction in the role of anti-war activist who can still admit to the subtle satisfactions of affection and comradeship that happened during his military career.

New converts can be trying. After the initial—often painful—self-confrontation, the air on the path of integrity can be heady. It is not unusual for someone in the early stages of self-discovery to have little tolerance for those who are caught in acts of conformity, rationalization, hiding or dissembling. It is well to remind yourself not to be too fast to rip off another person's mask. If the mask bothers you a lot, it may have something to do with an as-yet-unexplored part of yourself. A seasoned traveler on the integrity path is apt to have a mixture of compassion and distaste when confronted with another person's self-deception. While there are politically conservative gays as surely as there are revolutionary gays, gay people as a group tend to be tolerant of differences in other people. It is symptomatic of having come to terms with previously unacceptable parts of self. It does not mean that gays are without morality—far from it—they are just more willing to let other people grow and change too.

When one is far enough along the path of integrity to allow for other individuals' different styles of growth, there is compassion for the person who lacks integrity. Sometimes there is a friendly offer of a helping hand—maybe a question asked with humor. I recently saw someone on the street in my gay neighborhood handing out leaflets to inform people that Jesus would forgive them if they found the path back to heterosexuality through Christianity. He handed the pamphlet to two women who were strolling down the street with their arms around one another. They stopped and read it thoughtfully. One of them smiled and asked the man if he thought the best way to get started was to attend services at his particular church; he said that was why he was spending his day on the street. Then she asked why he thought homosexuality was bad and he said that he simply followed the words of Jesus. She handed the pamphlet back to him and gently suggested he might want to read the Bible again, remembering that Jesus had twelve male friends whom he loved and that he had never said anything to recommend this particular sect. She wished him a good life, put her arm around the other woman, and continued walking up the street. Nicely done. She was sure of her integrity and gave him a friendly jostle that he could use to develop his own integrity.

Dignity reflects an inner knowledge that you can face yourself in the mirror because you know more and more about yourself and are willing to continue the process of discovery. You are free to be honest about yourself with others and do not persecute those who are not as strong as you. A person of dignity walks with sureness and humble awareness that there are endless parts of self to be explored in the future. A zealot lacks dignity. Dedication to a single truth blocks too many doors to self-awareness. Notice the prominent persecutors of gays. Like all persecutors through time, they show plenty of single-minded zeal but lack dignity.

For integrity to continue to develop, it must be fed with change and growth. This cannot happen if you do not experiment, take chances and make mistakes. It involves the willingness to exercise your right to be a fool and come up with mud on your face after a mistake. We are accustomed to hearing that it "takes a big person to admit a mistake." Well, it takes a person in search of integrity to willingly *risk* a mistake in order to learn.

It is possible to own and learn to love the fool who lives inside each of us. Kings and queens externalized the fool part of self in the person of the court jester. The jester was not there for amusement only, but to act out that questioning mistake-prone part of the royal person who could use information thus gained to achieve majesty. In return, the royal ruler bestowed the mantle of special privilege and respect on the jester. The fool in each of us is a necessary part of the whole and it is urgent that we learn to own and love that part of self.

Learning to own and love the fool within yourself is especially difficult for males in this culture—probably the most difficult for non-gay males. Males are taught from the cradle to *endure* and to present a sturdy image. We are taught not to cry or hide our eyes in embarrassment. We are taught to tough it out, making it appear that we know what we are doing at all times and that our clearsighted path is honorable and above question. We all watched a recent President of the United States live out that boy-script and observed the lack of integrity it had developed in him. If he had been able to admit being a fool and laughed at himself, the healing could have begun and the male population of this nation might have learned something.

The physician friend who likes to take his hand puppet, Dr. Doctor, on rounds in the hospital while trailing the usual group of residents and medical students, is a prime example of a person who has overcome this deadly male training. His juniors are shocked to see him making such a fool of himself, though the more perceptive ones sense they are being taught that pomposity does not aid healing. He is gay and he has learned to question rules about how one is supposed to behave and feel. You sense that he does not mind if people are provoked to laughter by the fool in him. He knows why they are laughing. If they are laughing at him, it is a display of ignorance, and he has compassion for ignorance. And many are learning to laugh with him and expose their own internal fool.

If you are unwilling to be seen as a fool by others, how are you to experiment and develop integrity? Camp humor helps gay people to let out the fool. It often sheds light along with the laughter. A "who's *she* kidding?" when said by one gay male about another is often a reminder to stop trading on false male privilege in a world that uses privilege unfairly. The hundreds of "Dykes on Bikes" who led the 1977 San Francisco Gay Pride Day Parade were aware of the fool-humor of the play on words. It is the kind of fool-humor that makes you wonder. In this case, it made one wonder about gender roles and the meaning and use of power. It also stirred a first realization in some people that women, too, can be frightening and awesome.

The world is big, yet pulled together by a miraculous communication system. Everything that is happening in the world is happening to all of us. Gone is the cozy village of one hundred years ago where you knew your neighbors and change happened very slowly. Like Alice, we all have to run as fast as we can to stay in place. Some fall behind. People who cannot keep up with the accelerating social changes become dinosaurs in their own lifetimes and await death with unanswered questions in their gaze.

But most people, like most gay people, are capable of questioning themselves, exploring themselves, finding new truths, and integrating newly discovered parts into the evolving self that is strong and flexible. It involves risk and willingness to show yourself a fool. It involves learning from mistakes. It produces a person of dignity who deserves the respect bestowed by others.

From all of this comes satisfaction with your individual life—a sense of wonder mixed with contentment and happiness. It provides the quiet amid the chaos of our world. Integrity, dignity and the right to be a fool are the hallmarks of a human life well spent.

12

Exile?

The hatemongers are gathering momentum again. This is a collective manifestation of the dark side of human nature. We prefer not to look at that side of our nature and perhaps that is why periodic waves of hatred sweep a civilization. It forces the entire population to see that each of us is capable of evil as well as good, and that we are capable of venting our feelings of frustration, impotence, and rage in a bloodbath aimed at whichever neighbors seem least able to protect themselves. The rampage of hatred is usually thinly disguised as a wave of moral outrage, a social cleansing, not infrequently in the name of religious morality. We remember the Inquisition, the Salem witch hunts, Nazi concentration camps and gas chambers, and the McCarthy era. But here it comes again and too few people seem to recognize it because, while its banners still proclaim social reform, the target group this time is gay people. If the hatemongers were blatant enough to use Jews or blacks as their first target group, it would be more obvious where the campaign would lead. Let us remember that the Jews were not the only people in the

Nazi concentration camps during World War II. They were the largest and most publicized group. But, while some inmates wore the Star of David, some wore a pink triangle. They were the homosexuals.

Gay people have a good record of working to support the civil rights of all people, yet it is difficult to find needed friends when our civil rights are threatened. Within weeks of the time Shah Reza Pahlavi was driven from his throne in Iran by a revolution demanding *civil rights for all citizens,* the revolutionary Islamic government in Iran made no protest when religious courts established under the presumed rule of Ayatollah Ruhollah Khomeini began the persecution of homosexuals. In the city of Shiraz, six hundred miles south of Tehran, and in Tehran, seven men were shot by firing squads, convicted by religious courts on charges of "sodomy" and "raping" a male student, according to an Associated Press report. In Tehran, a newspaper report viewed the killing of gays as a sign of "hope for the future."

The current hate campaign in this country is aimed at gays, and the pious party line is that gays do not need any special protection of their civil rights. Hatemongers point out that we are sinners, that they are praying for us to change, that we an evil influence on the young, and that it is therefore sometimes justifiable to deny us equal rights in employment, housing, freedom of speech, and right of assemblage. Sound familiar? They are gaining ground with scare tactics reminding voters again and again to be wary because we prey on children.

One of the marching mottos was "Save Our Children." A very bitter irony there. Gay people usually have an awareness of gay identity as children, though they must wait until they are adults to do anything about it lest they be totally helpless outcasts in a prejudiced society. Young people lack the mobility to save themselves because they must remain under the "protection" of their parents until they are of adult age. Imagine yourself a gay child with adults all around you, perhaps including parents, enlisting in the hatemongers' crusade and talking constantly about how vile gay people are. It is the parents and other important adults who surround gay children with hatred that are killing their own children. And just in case there might be a respectable role model who could offer such a child some hope of survival, the hatemongers are trying to see to it that gay teachers, or any teacher who dares suggest gays have a viable life style, be fired. Of course, they will not stop with teachers. Next they will be after clergy, physicians, counselors, lawyers and any other respected group in the community. Their plan is to force respectable role-model gays, and those who dare speak of gay respectability, into silence and hiding. Imagine the chances of survival for the children lost in that sea of hatred! While injuring adult gays, the hatemongers will kill their own gay children first. It sounds primitive. Blood offerings are primitive. Hatred set loose in mobs with pious mottos is primitive. And it is frightening.

Perhaps we will be lucky this time. Perhaps enough people will realize that if you persecute one group of people and strip them of their rights, another "undesirable group" will be next until we are in another holocaust. Perhaps enough concerned citizens will wake up soon enough to realize that if one group is victimized in a society, no one is safe. We have seen it happen often enough in history. Enough California voters came to their senses to defeat soundly the Briggs initiative, which would have unleashed a statewide witch-hunt against teachers who are gay or who speak out in favor of gay people. But it is not at all clear why the measure was defeated. By election day the state's leading conservatives had joined the liberals and political moderates in denouncing the initiative. Some of these politicians are known to hate gays and would rightly deny that they are champions of humanism or civil rights. We must consider that they spoke out against Briggs' measure to checkmate a member of their own ranks whom they consider to be unstable and potentially dangerous to themselves. The voters did defeat the initiative, however, and showed some awareness that, if you begin to strip the rights of one group, any other group can be next.

For now the marching motto and demands of the self-righteous vigilantes do not sound sufficiently threatening to enough people. The voters in various American communities have simply required that gay people be silent, invisible and closeted once more. We are being told that we are to hide our "difference" and look like everyone else. Within my lifetime I have also heard people say that if only Jews were more "Christian" and blacks were more "white" there would be no problems. Gay people, as a group, cannot return to being silent, invisible and closeted. Some could try, but too many of us are too visible already. We are targets. And even for those gays who could, in theory, become invisible and closeted, there is that matter of integrity and the worth of human life.

Many of us choose not to sacrifice integrity and redevelop a bad self-concept. The bad old days lasted too long and, if we can do anything to keep them from returning, we will. We are being asked to abandon our identity. We are not simply defending a lifestyle, we are defending our lives! Without our lifestyle we cannot find one another. If we become invisible and divided, too many of us will be destroyed. It is a lesson that history teaches us from previous campaigns of hatemongers. "Repent," said the Inquisitor with Christian love as he tortured and destroyed those who were accused.

I wish that people could see that we gays are not the only ones endangered. How can anyone prove he or she is *not* gay or has not spoken in favor of gay people? Think about it.

Most gay people have had the experience of being exiles within their own nation. And that is an odd experience indeed. Imagine knowing that if you reveal your *feelings* you will be considered an outcast and run the risk of losing rights of citizenship. Imagine that if you reveal your *feelings* people may believe that they have the right to incarcerate you and administer shock treatments, drugs, or even physical mutilation such as lobotomies and castration. Imagine that. That is what it means to be an exile in your own land, growing up wary.

Exile. What an exotic word! When I was a youngster and had the usual bits and pieces of history tossed my way in school, it was one of the word pictures that stuck in my mind.

Perhaps I dimly realized that I might need to know more about that word one day. I pictured a person sent to an island to live alone, cut off from people as a punishment. Then I learned that exile often meant going to live in another part of the world. Again, I understood it to be a punishment. It was not until I was grown up that I began to understand all of the political reasons for exile. The phenomenon is usually related to the current rulers' fear of the free trade of ideas and ideology.

We have been invisible exiles in our own land, but in the last decade a large number of us have become visible. We are now estimated to be at least 10 percent of the population. That is a big minority. With more and more of us daring to become visible, the guardians of the status quo have joined the hatemongers in believing that "something must be done." What do they fear? That we will encourage other gay people to "come out" and become visible? Their fears are right on that count. Are they afraid that, if people see us as ordinary human beings who are capable of happy and satisfying lives, the hidden gays will also throw off the shackles of a non-gay lifestyle and join us? That fear is well-founded also. Are they afraid that everyone will join us? Is our lifestyle that attractive? Does it stir some desire in the hearts of the hatemongers? Do they suspect that they too at times have felt capable of loving someone of the same gender? Are they afraid they will be pulled from their private closet unless the gays are separated with thick walls?

Some non-gays are merely unthinking and insensitive. They have unquestioningly picked up the prejudices of the culture. It is insidious. I know an intelligent, well-educated woman who is a liberal and has given much thought to the cause of gays. She recently told her ex-husband, who is gay, that she has reservations about their teenage daughter living with him while in high school because, "I wouldn't want her exposed only to your one-sided way of life." As if it were possible with all public areas of life dominated by the 90 percent heterosexual majority, for a youngster to be "exposed only to your one-sided way of life!" And that from an intelligent, well-educated liberal!

But we must face the realities. Hate and fear can spread easily. Gays could be the first group stripped of their rights and forced into submission. But it will not happen quietly and it will not happen without a great deal of agony for both gays and non-gays. There are a number of outspoken gays who propose defensive violence. I am not one of them. But their view is understandable. They point to the long years of patient negotiation by black people (and the non-blacks who were concerned about the oppression of this group). They point out that it was not until shots were fired and buildings were burned that the general public sat up and paid attention. There is no denying these facts.

Violence may be a necessity in the fight for survival, especially when there is an active campaign to erase us. This is not a period in history when we are simply asking for equal rights. This is a period when the hatemongers are actively crusading against our right to exist.

My reason for not joining those who propose violence is that I believe we live in a society that is already too violent and in a violent period of history. I believe that violence begets violence. I do not believe that guns and explosives lead to peace. Guns and explosives kill and maim people. And all too often those who get killed and maimed are the innocent. Armies are better equipped to protect themselves. The have-nots in any society catch the brunt of violence because they cannot protect themselves when violence takes over.

But the temper of the times is such that I am sure we gays will protect ourselves and the geographical areas where we have congregated together in sufficient numbers to offer one another help. One day we may make our world sane enough that ghettos will be unnecessary and we can live in an integrated society. But today gay people, like other threatened minority groups, are drawn together in large cities because it makes us feel more safe. We do have gay ghettos. Ironically, they often turn into tourist meccas. The tour buses are amusing and they are an insult. I hope that the strategists of the hatemongers do not choose to bait us in our ghettos. The Warsaw ghetto was not that long ago and books and movies have brought its lesson home to younger gays. Baiting us in our ghettos could lead to major conflagration. I doubt that gays would then simply try to defend the ghetto until those who are left are taken away. We know now what the people in the Warsaw ghetto did not know. In order to defend our territory we would have to reach out offensively into other areas of the city and nation. And there are plenty of gays who were schooled in military killing factories. The know-how is there. We have little or no control over where and how the hatemongers choose to attack us. I hope for the sake of everyone that they do not try to take away our ghettos.

More moderate leaders in the gay community are urging that we plant ourselves firmly, aggressively seek our rights in the courts, make ourselves visible in nonviolent demonstrations, and ride out this wave of insanity. But they too admit that we must not bow meekly to violent attack on our persons and property. If it comes to fighting, we must defend ourselves by the most aggressive and efficient means available. Since we are only 10 percent of the population, they suggest that nonviolent displays of strength and unity will bring the reasonable non-gays to our side. We cannot take on National Guard units and hope to win (even though it would cause the nation as a whole to sit up and pay attention to what was happening). Moderate leaders recommend nonviolent retaliation as long as it does any good, but if we see that we are being ground under, we must use other strategies.

Some of us can disappear. Our lack of visibility can be used as an asset. We can blend with the rest of the population and seem to behave just like heterosexuals. Unless the witchhunt becomes massive and aggressive, as it was for the Jews during Hitler's reign, the invisible ones can last out the ten or fifteen years that it usually takes for sanity to return. Others who are already too visible would have to go underground and/or leave the country. We will win our struggle for equal rights eventually because the consciousness of the world is being awakened.

The moderate strategy is to minimize violence and have as few martyrs as possible during this period of madness. Perhaps it will be the gays of this country who one day lead us back to the vision of the founders of our nation, who believed there was richness and diversity and that *different* kinds of people could live together in one nation in peace and harmony. We have been at it only two hundred years. We may make it yet. The Vietnam War escapees are still watching from the sidelines in other nations. They were disloyal to the national rules of the moment but loyal to moral conscience. Perhaps we can make room in our nation for people whose conscience forces them to admit a mistake. Before we have pulled together into a pluralistic society we may all have to deal with our conscience and admit mistakes.

One thing we must do is try to understand the motivations of the hatemonger crusaders. Their foot soldiers are the people who feel as if they have been pushed around in society and have never been recognized as important individuals. Often, but not always, they are people of limited education. They are people who are vaguely dissatisfied and frustrated. The American Dream of success has not come true for them. They need someone to blame. They hate, and anger builds. Periodically the fascist-oriented, power-hungry, would-be leaders of a nation sense that this group has grown in number and that their collective mood is explosive. That is the time for such leaders to step in and point a finger at first one scapegoat target group and then another. "It's *their* fault. *They* are undermining your American Dream. *They* are the ones who undermine the morals of your children. *They* are the ones with all the money and property. Get them!" To keep the foot soldiers going, the finger is pointed at one group after another until the fascist leaders are firmly entrenched in power. The foot soldiers feel temporarily victorious since their leaders are in power, though as the years pass they find their frustration and anger growing once more because their dreams continue to elude them. The foot soldiers find themselves poorer in pocket and spirit than before.

In this current campaign of the hatemongers, the Bible is being clutched and waved about as it has been to justify other social horrors in the past. (It is even more useful in proving that women are inferior.) I wonder, at times, what would be used as ultimate justification if no such book of "rules" had been written. I suppose they would point to family rule books written by fathers and mothers. "My Daddy said it isn't right to be a homosexual and that women aren't as good as men, so there!" They are like children in dangerous adult bodies. Many of these people have serious psychological conflicts centered around authority. The "authority" is the ultimate justification, yet there is an inner urge to unseat the authority because they feel perpetually second-class. This authority conflict is harnessed by fascist leaders who provide absolute authority and divert the urge to destroy authority by pointing out scapegoat groups to attack.

These are people who fear their own sexuality. They have not explored their inner emotional world. They have not learned the difference between feelings and behavior. They have been taught not to recognize many of their true feelings because those feelings are "bad" and, if recognized, will be instantly translated into behavior. They have not learned how to control primitive impulses except with the fragile mechanism of keeping such impulses out of awareness. Everyone feels murderous anger at times. When you confront such feelings, you learn that you have sufficient self-control, that you can admit the feelings and find a means of venting them without actually killing. Everyone experiences feelings of lust. The more able you are to recognize the feelings, the more you learn that you are capable of diverting their expression and so do not have to sexually molest people on the street.

The foot soldiers of the hatemonger crusade tend to be people who try hard not to see their unacceptable feelings. They do not admit to murderous rage and certainly not to homosexual attraction. Without recognizing these feelings they have not had opportunity to exercise and trust their controls. Gay people threaten their primitive protection against their own feelings. We mirror their homoerotic desires— feelings of tenderness, woman for woman, man for man. Their fright is expressed as disgust. And they are easily tempted to destroy this mirror so that they need not look at the parts of self they have been taught are bad. Some seemingly sophisticated and well- educated members of society fall into this trap. Note the vehemence of some psychiatrists and clergymen when talking about homosexuality. Why would they feel so strongly about it if it were not threatening their personal defenses?

What about exile? What about physically leaving the country? I could do it if I had to. One hundred years ago it was difficult but necessary for people to pull up stakes and move from one part of this country to another. I have non-gay friends who have moved to other countries because they are more tranquil, or to reassure themselves that they can live in more than one culture and speak more than one language. Gertrude Stein and Alice B. Toklas chose France as their home, though they always thought of themselves as Americans. They were able to be themselves in France, to be respected for their contribution to culture, and not be viewed as freaks because of their lesbian love.

I would hate to leave the lovely climate and scenery of my adopted California. It was cold and bleak in the New Jersey winters, and I have come to love the West Coast with its kind gifts from nature. But I could leave if it were a choice of denying my integrity in order to enjoy the scenery. Hardest, of course, would be leaving my children and other loved ones. That is almost too painful to think about. I have to become hard and remind myself that if I am considered a bad person in this country I do them no good by staying. They will then be safer if I am located elsewhere. I hope they could visit me. And in a few years they would be old enough to join me if they wish.

I must remember that part of my parental responsibility is to be an example rather than to babble verbal instructions about how to live. My departure, though painful, would demonstrate that it is unnecessary to endanger one's life in a period of national hysteria—that it is not necessary to surrender dignity and integrity or to pay taxes to a nation that tries to destroy you. Why remain loyal when that to which you pledge loyalty subverts your life? To do so would be as stupid as the authority-conflicted clutchers of the Bible in this current wave of hatred. I want my children to see that I would rather wash dishes for income and learn a new language in a country where I can be myself than deny my identity in order to be a privileged member of this society.

And that would be my advice to all gay people who cannot fade into invisibility if the current wave of hatred becomes epidemic. Let us stay and confront them with nonviolence as long as it does any good and then let us leave. Keep your passports up-to-date and handy, and have an escape route planned. Let there be no concentration camps, "relocation camps," or "reeducation centers" this time.

Like the Jews, we gay people have been a target group too often in the history of the Western world. Maybe we need a homeland. I have sometimes had a wonderful fantasy that we could buy enough property and import enough voters to insure our rights in one state of the union. It could be our homeland—not restricted to gays, but open to non-gays who like us and appreciate a diverse society. We could assure the non-gays of non-discrimination in civil rights.

Since I find California attractive, I think, "Why not California?" We are already one out of three registered voters in San Francisco. We could concentrate on bringing more gay people to San Francisco, a very beautiful ghetto, and help one another to buy land and buildings until we own a clear majority of the city. From there we could spread to the rest of the state until we are a clear majority in the entire state. Let the other states then deal with us! We could offer safety to escapees from other states.

And, I would bet that we could teach the world a thing or two about building a pluralistic society. We have already demonstrated our ability to live with people different from ourselves. We have learned the hard way to be appreciative of differences.

It amuses me. If almost all the gay people in the nation were to migrate to California, how would the rest of the country survive? I think most Americans have very little idea how many of us tend their needs, not only as hairdressers and interior decorators, but also as teachers, clergymen, physicians, ambulance drivers, firemen, police, and so forth. A disproportionate number of us serve the needs of our fellow humans. Maybe it happened as a reaction to being told we were bad, having to prove to ourselves and others that we are good and useful. But my fantasy does amuse me. If we could collect in one state (living happily with non-gays who are not offended by us) and leave anti-gays to fend for themselves in other states, we might be fully appreciated at last.

My other advice to gay people in preparation for the holocaust that may come is to make yourself as flexible as possible. Learn at least one other language so that you can live elsewhere on the planet for a time if necessary. Try to develop other talents that can be used to earn a living so that you are not tied to one job. And experiment with simple living so that you know you can get by with very little money if you have to leave your property. It is not preparing for a picnic. A holocaust is no fun. But we can survive it. That is the important part. When it passes, we can come out of hiding and return from other lands and help the contrite nation to rebuild. Having spent its hatred, this nation may be ready to respect differences.

Living, loving, aging, and dying are more difficult in a foreign land. These aspects of life need the roots of home. But we must make our "home" portable. We must learn how to increase the quality of our contacts with one another so that home can be offered quickly in new settings. It is true that we are very diverse in our subgroups and we must learn better how to leap our own boundaries. Admission of our desire to love has made that possible. We must keep up our traditions and play harder at finding one another and offering love and support.

If we are to be exiles, we will see who loses most.

13

Ages and Stages

The idea of relating stages of development—physical, emotional, and intellectual—to a child's age was a great boon to pediatricians and child psychologists. But probably parents most needed the reassurance of a predictable pattern of development in what often seemed a sea of constant change. The notion of ages and stages helped us all to see the natural process of growth. The stage did not always match the age for an individual child, but we could see a general plan and understand some of the basic reasons for sudden change as the child developed. If the individual child was ahead or behind in some aspect of development, that could be understood and accepted. It could sometimes point to areas where the child might need help.

With our usual human naivete we did not immediately make the corollary assumption that people continue to change even after they have reached voting age. We had some dim awareness of emotional changes, and some bits and pieces of knowledge about intellectual and physical changes, but it took several decades for the social scientists to latch on to the obvious extension of the ages-and-stages idea and apply it to adults. We continue to change and develop from the moment of conception until a human life is finished.

Just as we learned with children that there is a subtle interplay of social, physiological, and emotional forces at work, we now begin to see these forces determining change in adults. As the idea of developmental stages once revolutionized our view of growing children, it is now revolutionizing our view of growing adults. Within the past few years, books like *Passages* by Gail Sheehy (Dutton, 1976) and *The Seasons of a Man's Life* by Daniel J. Levinson and others (Knopf, 1978) have focused excited public attention on the phenomenon. We do not stop growing and developing when we become adults. Maturation is a continuing process. And it is a comfort to maturing adults to know that some of the seemingly inexplicable changes they go through are shared by most other adults who may have been equally mystified and lonely in their changes.

Although Dr. Steven Morin and Dr. Dorothy Riddle broke new ground with an exploration of the developmental stages of gay psychologists reported in the November 1977 issue of the *A.P.A. Monitor*, we still have ahead of us the serious study of the developmental stages of cultural subgroups. Gay people, for instance, *as a group* have a pattern of developmental stages through which they move as they grow. We may be a group most worthy of study in helping social scientists and the general population understand the influence of subgroup identity within a culture. It is a three-dimensional model which is vastly more complex than the two-dimensional roadmaps we have developed so far. While the gay individual tends to follow the maturational path of adults in this society, he or she may start the developmental stages of gay maturation at any time of life. And, of course, *where* one starts will influence dramatically what happens. Beginning the maturation of gay identity at age eleven is quite different than beginning it at age fifty.

We are in need of serious research in this area and gay people understandably may not feel safe in being studied. Our experiences with social scientists and clinicians in the past were not pleasant. In our case, researchers forgot the presumed objectivity which is the foundation of the discipline. They began with the assumption that there was something wrong with us and then set out to find exactly what it was and how it came to be. We may take some convincing that we are, at last, assumed to be a natural variant or subgroup before we submit ourselves to study again.

Nevertheless, I would like to share a proposed model of gay maturational development that is based on my experiences with gay people whom I have known socially and clinically. It is an illustration of the three-dimensional model I believe necessary to understanding our maturational experiences. This is an educated guess and it is offered only as an illustration. But it is a beginning in understanding self-development for a gay person that could help us feel less lonely and mystified by the growing changes that we experience.

The mental picture that I have is that of a river. Like all rivers, there is a source and tributaries and a general flow toward the sea. The general terrain is different for each individual gay person. The stages and passages are predictable for the population as a whole. The model I propose has nine identifiable stages.

Dim Beginnings. Far back in the misty regions of awareness, where the terrain is not clearly visible and the thin air contains little consciousness, there are the first stirrings. There is an emotional pull toward people of the same gender, perhaps one individual in particular. There is something vaguely uncomfortable associated with these glimpses and stirrings. This is the source—the beginning of the river of gay identity. One breathes the cultural air of homophobia and assumes it is natural. The uncomfortable pull toward some individuals of the same gender is undeniable. You want to be near, perhaps to touch. You are stirred by voice, texture of skin, a mannerism. There may be abortive experiments and half-experiences. You may unknowingly invite a homoerotic approach and feel uncomfortable if the person tentatively obliges or feel insulted or misused, as if there were a strange case of mistaken identity. "Why does that person look at *me* that way?" This is the beginning of feeling different and alone. One is not apt to talk about it freely with others. There is an inner warning voice cautioning that some things are better left unexplored and unspoken. During this first period of dim beginnings, the person develops the rudimentary feelings of unsureness and the consequent rudimentary elements of strength, both of which will grow and develop through subsequent early stages and be visible in later periods of transition from one stage to the next.

Self-confrontation. The source has provided the beginnings and now the new river begins to flow. It is fed by small trickles that are its initial tributaries. There are experimental interchanges with other gay people during this period. The person may not yet be ready to announce herself or himself as gay, but is interested in other people who have some of the same feelings dimly perceived to be harbored within. Some degree of self-loathing may accompany increased admission of feelings to awareness. Slowly there is the dawning of a more full admission. "I do want to be closer to that person. That person is attractive to me. I do want to respond to that person's advance or invitation." There is a feeling of aloneness. "Are those other people who are called homosexuals like me? Who are my people and what are they like? Can I trust them?" The eyes are now open and more and more of "those people" appear as tributaries that touch and feed the river of awareness. Then the moment of truth. "I guess I *am* one. What will my life be like? Shall I try to hide and escape? No, I am who I am." This is the stage during which the burden is shouldered. The new river is running shallow but moving more rapidly. It has accepted its identity and its destiny, though neither may be clear.

The Private Self. The new river is moving now and since it is a river of human identity, there are persistent questions asked of self. "Who am I, anyway? Am I the person I have heard described as one of *them?* There are parts of me that are parts of the tributaries that have fed me. I have been touched by other gay people and find parts of them I like. I often feel related in some way. Where are the role models? Who are the gay people I want to be like? Where can I find them? Shall I keep my gay side separate and hidden and continue to live in the straight world? Will I be found out? Should I put all parts of me together and be one person with a sole identity? What will people think of me? What will I think of myself?" The gay identity is set but it needs to be refined. The river is moving rapidly now in narrow confines headed for unknown terrain that seems frightening.

Cutting Loose. The terrain is rocky, turning the river into rapids. It is the period of adolescence in the development of the gay person. Having plunged into what looks like the gay world with little previous experience that is helpful (and usually with no guidance), the path of the river is indeed rocky during this stage. Sex and love are actively explored. There are plenty of hurts and bruises and the developing person becomes more and more tired and alert. It is a period of active learning and sorting. People met during this period provide tips and types, some positive, some not. In the initial plunge, it may seem as if one has entered a candy store where no currency except desire is required. But there are times when the candy store seems more like a wax museum in which all are dead. Sudden love, once physiological passion is spent, can turn flat. There is a desperate desire to direct one's flow but the terrain is so full of surprises that mastery seems all but impossible.

Power and Peace. The rapids are left behind and the river slows as it reaches a leveling stage. This is a period of gaining mastery. One discovers that it is possible to direct the flow. The river is much wider now. Experience has helped. A self-portrait has developed. "I know who I am." A way of life becomes established. "This is the kind of person I am and this is the kind of gay person I am going to be." One learns during this period or stage which parts are the private person and

which parts are the public person. This does not mean that
the person remains closeted, but that one has learned when
and where it is appropriate to show all or part of one's feelings. The rapids taught its lessons about how to keep alive
and vital without constantly being bumped, bruised, or
turned this way and that without warning. This is the stage
during which feelings of self-respect flower. One learns com-
petence and how to flow with minimal wariness, knowing
there is strength in reserve. This is also the period of mature
mating. The waters of the river change from clouded fright to
clear awareness. Illusions become a luxury, used as an indulgence. The love relationship may last for a few months or
many years, but is always a source of learning during this
stage.

The Falls. The preceding maturational stage is apt to hit
sudden surprises. The river will be moving surely on its
course when the terrain suddenly changes; a sheer drop from
a mountainside can cause a waterfall that is breathtaking
and changes the river forever. The surprise of the falls can
come in many forms. There may be the environmental assault of a witch-hunt that threatens or destroys both economic and social security. A lover may leave. There may be a sudden unexpected infatuation with an unaccustomed and
unlikely sort of person. The body may fail and reveal a serious disease or malfunction. There may be a physical accident. There may be the death of a gay loved one. Coping with
these sudden surprising falls in life helps the person to learn
to draw on the strengths of the inner self. Depending upon the
resources found within, one is apt to become more or less dependent upon others.

Meaning and Depth. After a fall, there is a period of reas-
sembling. The separated parts of the river flow back into itself but the river has changed. Some questions asked and answered during the preceding two stages must be asked and
answered again. "Who am I now? What do I do with these
changes of setting, job, love life, friends? What are my goals
now?" The river moves with more strength now. The gay

person has a much better sense of self. There is more depth to the person and life has clearer meaning. It is the middle age of gay development. There is sureness based on experience. Illusions are dissipated. Bitterness and hurts are put in perspective. There is a new sobriety in the sense of self. There is a heightened self-acceptance and understanding of the world. There is an awareness of one's own rhythms and motivations, whatever surprises the terrain may hold in store. Love relationships during this period peak in maturity. Love is taken as it is, two individuals who share something greater between them, alone but together. More time is spent alone with greater satisfaction. There tend to be fewer friendships but they are characterized by more understanding, depth and openness. It is during this stage of the gay person's development that the meaning of life is defined.

A Period of Vision. The end of the journey is in sight. The gay person is apt to turn back and sort memories during this period so that the beginnings are equally in sight. What has it all meant? This stage of life is a preparation for the final phase. The person's gay identity has long since been accepted and there is more perspective on the hue and cry surrounding the phenomenon of gayness. The gay person at this stage of life is often striking in the effortless acceptance of nature and its variations. It is a period of final accounting. There is a willingness to help others, particularly other gay people, counterbalanced with an awareness of personal limitations. Last, it is the period of final remediation. During this stage, the gay person makes up what has been lacking in life or understands that it will not be made up.

Final Flow. The smell of the sea is in the air and the journey's end within reach. The body is apt to be frail and the spirit strong. The gay person, having fought individualistically through life, is not likely to settle for a nursing home— more often preferring to die a little sooner. This is the stage of quiet knowing. There is awareness that the end is the beginning. River will merge with sea. And the sea will feed the clouds that take moisture to new sources. It is at this stage of life that the gay person is able to look through the bigot, knowing more than can be said.

I find this model of gay developmental stages interesting, and it helps me to keep the movement of the gay individual in perspective. But it is more complex when utilized to understand an individual's path and progress, because it must be superimposed on the developmental stages of the general population in our culture.

Imagine, for instance, meeting a gay man in his early fifties who started his gay development later than the average person and is now in the fourth stage, cutting loose. Superimposed on his established mature life is the adolescence of his gay development. With gray hair and a sterling reputation in his community, he now sets forth to explore love and sex with a vengeance. Some people are apt to think he has lost his mind and communicate that vision to him. Yet what he is going through is perfectly normal if you realize there are two developmental tracks being followed at once.

Or let us take the gay woman who discovered near her thirtieth birthday that she had a terminal illness that would permit ten more years of life at most. She started her gay identity young and it speeds up now to aid her in this time of stress. When you meet her, she is thirty-five years old and in the final stage of gay development, the final flow. She is making active decisions about employment, early retirement, financial provisions that will help her lover to retain the house they built together, and preparations for this early departure from her lover. There are things to be done. She is alert and lively but there is also the quiet knowing in her eyes along with the failing body and the strong spirit. She is coping with sexual needs, as would anyone her age who is dying of a degenerative disease, but she has coped before. The quiet sureness of the final phase of gay development would seem eerie in a woman of this age if you did not know she was gay and had already run her developmental course as a gay person.

And there are the not-so-happy fits of two developmental paths. I am thinking of the man in his early thirties who has achieved professional status after a long hard climb. His gay developmental level did not fit well with his level of development as a male in this culture. In gay development he had just reached the stage of the falls. Barely arrived in his struggle to become a man, as our culture defines it, and having been for some time in the power and peace phase of gay development, he was suddenly struck by illness, the loss of employment, and the loss of a lover. Had this happened to him earlier or later in his life, he might well have grown in strength as a result. But it was an unfortunate coincidence that these two stages of development coincided. He was unable to move on to the next gay developmental stage of meaning and depth. He was too unsettled in his gayness just as he was getting a grip on the settling-down stage of American manhood. After tortured attempts to cope that were accompanied with repeated failures, he ended his life with suicide.

It is a blessing and a curse to be following two developmental paths at the same time. It can add depth and strength, or it can create confusion that undermines one's sureness of self. It can help one to develop agility but it can also create immobility. Probably, if we were better informed about how both developmental programs work, we would be better able to reach out and help those in trouble.

We need to understand more about how developmental stages work for people in other subgroups of our culture also. How does it work for black people? How for Orientals or Chicanos? How is it different for women and men? What if one is a gay Oriental woman? How do the three developmental programs interact?

We are learning. Perhaps one day we will be willing to invest in studies that help us learn to help each individual's river run safely to the sea rather than telling people how their river should flow.

14

Season Within Season

Many authors and philosophers before me have compared the seasons of nature with the seasons of human nature. I notice that we humans, like the rest of nature, show a preference for privacy and intuition in the first and final seasons of our life while the middle two seasons are more open to inspection. Also, as in nature, our first seasons seem to be more colorful until you notice the subtlety of the final seasons.

My daughter, Vicki, is a source of pride and joy for me and has been since the day she was born. She is fourteen now and I am forty-eight. We are certainly in different seasons, but we have a lot in common and I am learning from her. Both of us are caught up in seasons within seasons. Any observer of nature has noticed that there are seasons within seasons—some of them transitions, some a necessary change of weather or mood. Vicki and I are both in periods of transition, she finding her own way into something that relates to our cultural concept of adolescence, me finding my way into a change of lifestyle. She seems to do it more gracefully than I, admitting and riding her feelings while I tend to count to three and hold my breath before plunging into the next wave.

We have had an unusually close relationship all of these years and it is helping us now. Both of us are turning more of our energy and attention in other directions, consciously discussing the necessity of this kind of separation that permits us to be going on our individual ways while keeping the close emotional bond. I feel fortunate that we have always both insisted on keeping all communication lines open because they are serving us very well now.

The culture dictates appropriate behavior and emotions for men and for women (different) within each season of life. Once again, gay people have been more fortunate in having been shut out of the cultural mold so that they have had to try to create some sort of individually satisfying blend of behavior and emotion for their seasons. Some of us have not been terribly successful, but the opportunity has been there and almost all have tried—some with stunning success. But neither the population at large, nor gay people as a subgroup, have been prepared for the season within season. It seems odd because, while the timing of their arrival cannot be predicted, the fact of their arrival can be. This phenomenon has been called to my attention again and again in my clinical work. It has also been called to my attention in my personal life.

The fact that Vicki and I are in similar transition periods, or seasons within seasons, right now was brought home to me recently during a potluck party given by my lover for his graduate students. It was also a sort of housewarming for our new shared abode. Vicki had a longstanding family friend who is a few years older visiting overnight and the two of them asked if they could be bartenders. Since the choice of drinks was red wine, white wine or mineral water with lemon or lime, and since I knew she wanted some definite role at the party, I gladly agreed.

Midway through the evening, the rug was rolled back when some hot current disco music was put on the stereo and both Vicki and I slipped temporarily into new roles. She asked me to tend bar while she raced for the dance floor. I was delighted because it made me look busy while watching her dance. Within a couple of minutes, I could see that the graduate students were intimidated by this energetic fourteen-year-old who had labored hard to learn the newest dances. Several fell into line behind her and started learning. The rest drifted back toward the wall to watch. It was not until the music had stopped and they applauded that she self-consciously realized she had been an attraction and produced a lovely blush. The little girl had been a young lady and a star.

While she was dancing, a slightly inebriated young woman came to the bar and told me she loved the way I had decorated the house. I had been a husband in suburbia long enough to notice a compliment aimed at a wife when I heard one. I smiled. "Your daughter is quite a dancer," she went on.

"It must be in the blood," I smiled, trying to make pleasant chitchat. "I taught dancing once upon a time." (Dancing was a true passion in my youth and I earned money teaching social dancing while in college and even in the Army.)

The young woman seemed unsure where to carry the conversation. "Do you still teach dancing?" she asked.

"No, that was a while back," I said smiling socially once again.

Pause. "Do you work?" she asked. Another remark too often aimed at a wife! I could hardly believe my ears. I said that I was a psychologist and was saved further inquisition by my daughter's ovation and her hasty return to resume her less conspicuous role tending bar.

I scooted for the kitchen to regain my emotional balance where I was asked by someone if I had the recipe for "that delicious salad you prepared," just before a departing male guest came in, shook hands, and said, "Hi, I haven't had a chance to say hello. You're the other. . ." Pause.

"Host," I supplied.

He blushed slightly and seemed ill at ease. "Right! The

other host. We're just leaving and I wanted to say thanks. You don't know me but I'm Jane's wife—I mean *husband!*" Large blush.

Lots of sex role troubles that evening. I was surprised but did not mind. In truth, I was more than a little amused. I have never been treated like a wife before. I am sure it would become trying as a steady diet but it was interesting. My lover, our offspring, and I all had a good laugh about it at the breakfast table and I remembered again that Vicki and I are both in transition.

Because we have had no training for it, it is difficult for us to honor transitions. Somehow you must get the knack of blending old and new behavior, stepping back far enough to get some perspective and not losing your balance. It is not an easy act. Too often a client or friend has confided that they find it particularly troublesome because they feel discomfort similar to the feeling of doing something wrong or being in a slump. It seems to be very comforting to have someone point out that you are having a transition period, a season within a season, and that you need emotional time and space to permit the innermost emotions to sort and formulate.

Sometimes in the office I feel more like a nineteenth-century physician than a twentieth-century psychologist when I ask if a client cannot get some time off from work and take a trip somewhere. I am apt to remind people when they are experiencing a season within a season that nature is a great teacher. It offers timelessness, quiet, and the reassurance that change is natural and constant. In the rare instances when it is not possible to take some time away in mountains, desert, or beach, we try to figure out some other change of scenery—like a lunchtime walk to the top of a hill for several days. It is one time when the emotional nutrition is more important than the food.

Honoring these periods of transition is not usually a matter of problem-solving. It is a matter of finding a way to stop fretting about the altered state within, letting it take care of itself. Nature helps at these times. It rarely gives direct instruction. but it calms you while your own inner process gets on with what it needs to do.

I think these constant shiftings, with seasons within seasons, are very necessary. Too much sameness flattens and encases life in such a way that natural change and growth are difficult without major eruption. The seasons within seasons keep you emotionally fluid. It is the essence of life, the harsh mandate of nature: Grow or wither; use it or lose it. We have all seen too many people who have lost it, couples who sit staring at one another and the walls in a restaurant with nothing left to say, individuals who do not know what to do with vacation time.

Of course, there is risk. What else is new in life? The risk is felt most keenly when there is a partner or spouse. I recently bade farewell to a client who was making a pilgrimage to his family and the scenes of his childhood, because for two years he had intuitively known he must go back there to get a sense of the flow of his life and how it had all begun. But he had been immobilized by a cycle of depression and elation that was tied in with his relationship with his lover. They loved one another and wished the best for one another but when my client would get energized and ready for his trip and other adventures, his lover would be worried by the change of mood and wonder aloud whether he should dare such a major undertaking as the trip when his mood might change along the way. When my client was down with the blues, his lover was attentive and eager to help. That sort of system gets easily entrenched. My client was not honoring an important season within his season and the continued denial of his own natural growth process was slowly robbing him of life.

When there is a partner or spouse, the art of negotiation must be mastered. To tell a lover that you are changing in some important way is to threaten the security of the relationship. Talking it out together is the only way to discover how each partner can grow while letting the relationship grow and change in the ways that it must. These negotiations do not insure that the relationship will be a primary one for-

ever. Nothing can guarantee that. There are too many variables involved in human change. But avoiding the negotiations, and avoiding the evolution of personal seasons, is a
sure way of killing whatever life the relationship may have.
You may stay together bodily in the same environment for a
lifetime, but individual selves will have gone elsewhere.
Grow or wither; use it or lose it.

Nor need one be unduly frightened as the years move along
by the prospect of solitude. Gays have faced that prospect all
their lives and have learned to permit it less power to rule
their lives. May Sarton, in her personal journal *The House by
the Sea* (Norton, 1977), talks of the richness of living in solitude. She says the only times in her life that she can remember being "bone lonely" were when she was in love with
someone. In solitude, one can come to very comfortable
terms with oneself and nature.

We must learn to trust ourselves. The internal, often non-
conscious, workings of your mind and spirit will take you
where you need to go if you do not tangle the path with a lot
of "shoulds" and "should nots," most of them learned when
you were too young to reason for yourself and taken from a
recipe for life that yielded satisfaction for no one. Most such
rules have to do with building a society and keeping untrust-
worthy natives in check. If you have been a responsible and
moral adult who takes the responsibility for thinking over the
genuine moral implications of your behavior, using a personally forged value system to weigh and measure, you should be
able to take a chance on trusting yourself. Of course,
sometimes you will be wrong and have to admit to being a
fool or having made a mistake. But you can also admit to trying. You can admit to being alive. You can admit to learning.
And nine times out of ten, when such a mistake is made, it is
because you have cluttered your path with a belief about
what you *should* do rather than paying attention to what you
must do.

It is hard to see how, if you let your own seasons (and
their seasons) roll by while trusting your inner truth to carry

you along your individual path, you could have any complaints. That master storyteller, Somerset Maugham, was full of complaints in the later years of his life, according to his biographers. At the root of it was his denial of his own homosexuality for too many years. And yet, he did apparently have a satisfactory loving relationship with another man for many years. But neither his adventure into heterosexual marriage nor his long-term relationship with a lover met the standards of the proper society that surrounded him. He was adored as an author and celebrity, but was alone in his misery. He made the mistake of not following his own path and missed the satisfaction that was right there in front of him.

I know two people these days who are not doing that. Both are attorneys—one in his fifth decade of life and one in his fourth. The first has chucked a successful career as a professor of law and has opened a nonprofit law practice dedicated to working for the legal rights of gay people. His mother, who lives near him and has seen him through a life of many changes, looks at him with marvel and tells him she has never seen him look better. After years of hiding his gay identity as best he could, he decided to follow his own inner wisdom several years ago. He has made mistakes, but tells me he has never been as happy as he is now.

The younger attorney is just beginning to follow his own inner truth. He has not made his disclosure to his family as yet, fearing rejection. But that is on the agenda and he knows it. On a recent visit he said "It seems to me that here I am at thirty-five, however I am, with parts of me a teenager, parts of me about five years old, parts of me an adult, parts of the gay me in wholeness, and all of me in transition all the time." Seasons within seasons. He smiled, "Want to know something? I'm glad to be here."

Which reminds me that I have known only one gay person in my lifetime who would have liked to go back to an earlier period in life. In contrast, I have known a number of nongays who wished they could be transported back to some earlier, happier period of life. I do not know what it means, but I think it may have something to do with our having accepted the fact that nature will have its way. Almost all of us have had some experience trying to be what we are not by nature. Almost all of us have found so much more happiness and satisfaction in being who we are. I guess we trust nature and know that we are a part of it.

I am thinking about Vicki's dancing again. She really is good. Maybe I'll take a few dancing lessons to get myself up-to-date and then go off to a few discos in style. Imagine me taking dancing lessons. The "should" voice within says, "You're too old. And besides you used to teach dancing yourself—why would you want to take lessons from some youngster?" The inner truth says, "I like dancing!" You cannot argue with inner truth.

15

Old at Heart

A young gay man of wit and charm, when asked what he wanted to be when he grew up, said "I want to be a dirty old man. How come I grew up with the myth that gay people are sex-crazed animals who live life from orgy to orgy, and now that I'm a grown-up gay person with a healthy body and libido, I find myself surrounded by a lot of talk and not much action? Everybody's so busy all the time! When I'm old, I'm going to make sure I have lots of time to go chasing."

Most myths have a seed of truth. If sex is defined broadly as awareness of one's body self and awareness of the body self of others, then it may be true that gay people are more occupied, if not preoccupied, with matters of sex. We notice one another more, are alert to sexual nuance in conversation, touch one another more, and enjoy being touched and admired. Perhaps we retain our awareness of sexuality throughout our lives more than non-gay people do. Maybe we just do not give up as easily.

Our part of the world has some weird ideas about aging. We are caught up in the worship of youth, though that worship rarely extends beyond matters of body attractiveness and sexual vitality. Of course this is going to change as the median age of the population continues to climb. One can see signs of the change already in the ages of the models pictured in advertisements. Seventeen-year-olds are on their way out and older folks are making their entrance. My favorite symptom of this change was a full-page advertisement in the *New Yorker* a couple of years ago that pictured Lillian Hellman draped in a luxurious coat with the simple statement at the top of the picture, "What becomes a legend most?"

The advertising agency was aware that not too many such expensive coats were going to find their way to the shoulders of seventeen- or twenty-seven-year-olds. Perhaps in a few years the same picture could carry the statement, "What becomes beauty most?" We are not quite there yet, but it will come. We will learn to see the beauty of age as well as we now see the beauty of youth. Old beauty is different from young beauty—not better, not worse, just different. There are beautiful young bodies and beautiful old bodies. There are beautiful young people and beautiful old people. The beauty resides only partly in the body, the rest is what shines through—qualities of openness, honesty, desire, hope, acceptance and generosity.

I keep hearing the refrain of that dreadful song that Frank Sinatra has crooned through too many of my car radios, ". . . if you are among the very young at heart . . ." I have seen too many older people insulted by well-meaning youngsters who tell them they are really swell because they are "young at heart." It has forced me to tell more than one young person that I feel disappointment because I can sense they are not *old* at heart.

Maybe it would help if we take a closer look at what it means to be young and old in our part of the world. Maybe the way gay people have learned and are learning to deal with old and young in our subculture could help some other people to reorient their thinking on this important subject. Remember, we are all growing old. That does not mean that death is imminent necessarily, but that we are headed toward increasing maturity. Old age has been so devalued in our society that old people lose their resources from despair over the unreal world in which they are sequestered. There is a sorrowfully accurate picture of the process described by Liv Ullmann in her book *Changing* (Knopf, 1977), in which she describes her grandmother: "The year when I was seventeen in Oslo, my best friend was seventy-five." She describes her grandmother's move in later years to an old people's home and, finally, to the nursing home annex where she was allowed no personal possessions and could only stare at blank walls and retreat back through memories to an unreal world that was less painful than the sterile reality in which she had been placed. Until they were separated, it was probably Liv's youthful companionship that helped her grandmother retain her lively interest in life. Likewise, it was probably the deep touching of intellect, heart and body by her grandmother that helped young Liv develop the depth that surfaced so early in her acting career.

In my experience *young* no longer means naive and wet behind the ears, if it ever did. And young is certainly not synonymous with beauty. *Old* no longer means feeble, incompetent or old-fashioned, if it ever did. And certainly old is not synonymous with ugly. There are bodily changes with time. Skin and muscle tone change—so do attitude and understanding, sometimes for the better and sometimes for the worse. Change is inevitable, but beauty and worth seem to have more to do with how one manages the changes.

As to young-at-heart versus old-at-heart, I suppose the former implies being unspoiled and adventuresome while the latter implies something like being receptive, patient, knowledgeable and having inner depth. We all have met people of all ages who would fit into either or both categories. Everyone grows up eventually, but not everyone grows onward and becomes more of a person.

Though segregation on the basis of age as well as color, social position, and in-vogue body beauty happens in the gay community, these lines are crossed over much more frequently than in the community at large. Sexual and general attraction have traditionally been pursued more freely by gay people and the pursuit has created the crossing of usual barriers. A young gay woman may be attracted more often by older women. She introduces them to her age mates who would not otherwise seek them out and some friendships are formed. A gay man may be especially attracted to Orientals and likewise introduce them to his Caucasian peers, again creating an occasional friendship that might otherwise not have happened. That is why one is more apt to see a mixture of ages and skin colors at a gay social event than at a non-gay social event. This is an enriching by-product of our lifestyle.

Let me try to say what it is I search for in older and younger people, and how it helps me to meet my needs and become myself. Perhaps you will find similarities and differences in your own search to answer your needs and it will help you to clarify your interaction with the phenomenon of age.

I find that as I grow older I have less quick energy. My tempo is slowing and I found value in this change. When I look back over past decades of my life, it seems as if I was moving so rapidly, trying to achieve, trying to "get there," that I did not see much of the scenery along the way. I walk more often than run now, and am able to notice things like the contour of a landscape or the feeling of the sun's warmth on my body that would have gone unnoticed earlier. I used to be very busy looking for the possibilities that were open to me. Now, in middle age, I know that there are more than enough attractive possibilities and I must move more slowly in order to experience the satisfaction.

Aging is providing me with more stability and perspective, but I am only in the middle years of my life. I know that I still move too fast. This is what I see in older people, the ones who are old at heart. I am drawn to their depth of inner security and the breadth of their perspective. I am also drawn to their experience. The more old-at-heart the person, the more she or he is able to draw on rich memories and can show me times when the world was different. As they share their past, they also teach me how they got to be who they are today. That is fascinating and useful information for me. It helps me to guide my life in these new times and places.

And I am attracted to them bodily when they are truly old at heart. The wrinkles in the skin and the softness of muscle, even the scars, have stories to tell. Not all of the stories can be told with words, but when you touch and listen quietly with your heart, you hear. You can absorb much of who the person has become and learn about the becoming through touch. Absorbing their truth this way helps me to feel my body changing, the ways in which it is becoming. With someone old at heart, I feel safer and more secure.

And with the young? I can re-experience the reckless joy of their speed, the willingness to run through the world and leap sudden chasms. With someone young at heart, I can re-experience the wonder of so many facets of life that are new. When I am with someone young at heart, I remember feeling sturdy, unsure, willing to risk, and full of possibilities. The bodily attraction has to do with the smoothness of skin and firmness of muscle. It is living sculpture a perfect blossom about to burst into flower. Through touch, you can listen to feelings they do not yet have the words to express. You can hear the silent request for nurturance and security and the disarming pride in the body that is offered to your touch. Communicating with someone young at heart through touch helps me to remember and incorporate parts of me that were never fully developed in my own youth.

I am talking about young people who are young at heart and old people who are old at heart. Not all young people remain young at heart and they have not developed as yet into someone old at heart. Some young people give up their youth and plod joylessly through life. Some old people have not grown old at heart though they long ago lost youth. They move from task to task with little understanding or depth. The gifted people are those who cross the age line within themselves—the young ones who are in touch with their aging and the old ones who retain something of their youth.

Some wonderful older people have helped to put me in touch with my growing old. While I am still in the in-between years, I savor the signs of my growing old. I realize that I am beginning to have more of what I wanted from life when I was younger. I am more able to go my own way and set my own rules. Because I have more experience behind me, I can see the rich array of options and choices open to me. If I want to travel now, I have a better idea of the places I want to visit and why. When I want the relaxation of a drink, I can choose a bottle of Perrier water and savor its taste as it reminds me of the water in France or sitting and drinking a special glass of water in Greece. There are the memories to draw on that make the *now* moment more rich. I listen to music more carefully and choose a particular symphony, aria, or *fado* that suits my need at the moment. I can select from a wider variety of foods when I want to eat and be more aware of how much I want to eat for maximum enjoyment. I can plan to watch a sunset and not despair if something happens and the plan must be changed, because I know there is tomorrow. I can reach out to comfort a loved one who is ill and offer the particular kind of comfort he or she will most appreciate.

Growing old at heart enables one to admit mistakes and regrets. I can remember falling hopelessly in love with a straight man before I was willing to admit to myself that I was gay. I can remember the lonely wasted childhood years in school where I was tortured more often than taught. I can remember times when I was not completely honest with my wife, or my lover, or myself, and regret that I was not more conscious and open to the consequences of honesty.

Admitting the mistakes and regrets of the past helps one to become more compassionate as one grows old at heart. Other people have their mistakes and regrets also. We are no better than we are, and we do what we believe we must do. It becomes easier to feel another person's feelings.

What about sex? One of the myths prevalent in our culture is that one loses sexual drive and interest as one grows old. Research on human sexuality and the sexuality of gay people in particular indicates that sexual needs run your life less as you grow older. The need for orgasmic experience is less and less urgent. Orgasmically-oriented sexual experiences become less frequent and sexual experiences in general become more deeply satisfying. It is the difference between running swiftly across a meadow and walking slowly across the meadow while noticing the grass and wild flowers. Those who are old at heart have learned to savor sexuality.

Perhaps the best gift that comes with growing old at heart is that it is less necessary to be a man or a woman. You can be a person. The strict directives of our culture for proper manly and womanly behavior are aimed at the young and middle-aged. Old people are people. It is not shocking for an old man to be sentimental and tender nor is it shocking for an old woman to be stern and powerful. You can be everything you are, finally, with minimal interference from the keepers of the code. Alice B. Toklas is an example of such a woman. While Gertrude Stein lived, Toklas devoted herself to the care, feeding and protection of her genius lover, much like a devoted wife. After Gertrude's death, Alice lived devotedly with her memory of Gertrude but she became an increasingly assertive person in her own right. She even developed as a writer and consultant to other artists. She was still both a woman and a lesbian but these labels no longer defined her. She became a person.

Sociologists have been telling us for a long time that we need to mix our generations. Segregation of people by age is costing our society dearly. The young, the middle-aged and the old are shockingly separated into communities that permit little interchange. And it is not simply a matter of housing. Even when the town looks integrated because people of all age groups live on the same block, they spend their time in different activities and socialize with their age mates or not at all.

Gay people have been somewhat more successful in breaking out of this mold. We probably have the same percentage of intergenerational pairings—though a seventy-year-old settled into a lasting relationship with a thirty-year-old is less shocking in the gay community than in the general community. Such a pairing, by the way, works well when it works because the chronologically younger person is old at heart while the older person is young at heart, and it makes for a lovely interplay of forces and brings much richness to the relationship.

How can we mix the generations if they are now so segregated? If you find that you are most attracted to older people, let yourself go and pursue some older people. Find the ones you are most drawn to and bring them back into your peer circle and introduce them. If you find you are most attracted to people who are younger than you, go after them, find the best ones and bring them back to meet your peers.

Won't people think it strange? Of course they will. Change is always perceived as strange and direct assault on unquestioned taboos always makes people uncomfortable.

Won't people think that there is something kinky going on? They will be right in thinking that something sexual is going on. Whether or not there is any sexual intercourse involved in the relationship, general attraction involves some nuances of sexuality. For once, current slang is accurate: when you are "turned on" to someone, you are attracted to all of the person, not just the brain or the genitals. If you are interested only in a person's mind you are missing a lot, since the activity and products of that mind are intimately bound up with the rest of the person. When you ignore the sexual aspects of the other person, you cheat yourself because sexual feelings will go into hiding.

Why not touch? Our society is so pathetically perverse in its aversion to any sort of touch that goes beyond ritual. Yet we are a society of people starving for touch. The massage movement that has been slowly flowering across the nation in the past ten years reveals the need. People are daring to touch one another and discovering the benefits of touching and being touched. The need for this sort of skin contact and its primitive reassurance does not end when one leaves the cradle. People stay fully alive longer when they touch and are touched caringly.

Depending upon your position in society, the amount and types of touching you may be permitted if you explore your touch needs may be limited in the beginning. But you may be able to start off with a shoulder rub after a swimming party. Even the slow, sensuous application of suntan lotion can be a beginning. Foot rubs are a little more exotic but you can point out that the Bible mentions them. Back rubs with clothes on feel wonderful if you have had little touching. But it is like taking a bath with your socks on. Naked, skin-to-skin, full-body rubs are the most transporting and nourishing, though it may take quite a while for your friends to get past the adolescent giggles and dirty jokes that mask their anxiety about having a secret need met so directly.

But the touching is wonderful and it breaks down the walls that separate us generationally and as people. When I touch an older person, I am often touching parts of me that I hope to become. Their experience rubs off in the silent interchange of skin against skin. And when an older person massages me, I can feel their interest and caring in the touch. I can sense that I am giving them something and that makes me feel good. I feel protected and cared for. After the massage, the barriers are down and I am better able to listen and am more open to their counsel.

When I am the older person touching a younger one, I find that I am often filled with tenderness and desire. In part, I touch the me that once was and I am able to touch the me that never had a chance to be. When the barriers are down, after the touching, I am more able to share my past and present and let them take of it what they will. And I can listen more clearly to their hopes and dreams after they have touched me. In the intergenerational rubbing of body and soul, something is exchanged. You are never the same. Something of the other person does rub off!

I notice that there is more intergenerational touching going on among gay people than there was half a decade ago.

Somehow we have learned its value. Even at the baths, which used to be strictly flesh markets where the sexually desirable were too quickly devoured, young and old touch each other in passing more often now and, more often, there is a moment of lingering—a sense of something being exchanged between the two people in the moment of their touching. At very least it is a recognition that the old were once young and the young are growing old and that we all need one another.

I must not end this chapter without attacking the myth that old and gay means old, miserable and lonely. In an article entitled "Patterns of Aging," by Douglas C. Kimmel, which appeared in the November 1977 issue of *Christopher Street*, he reports on some preliminary research on the aging experiences of gay men.[1] It turns out we tend to be less wasted and less lonely. Perhaps it is because we have had fewer role restrictions. Gay people learn to do for themselves. A gay man can do necessary sewing and cooking and a gay woman is able to change a fuse or a flat tire. We have learned how to entertain ourselves and make life worth living without the ready-made focus of children and family. That sort of learning lasts into old age, so that the gay person tends to be more active and more satisfied with the quality of life as an old person. Old age sometimes does carry real problems, both for gay and non-gay people. Help may be needed in finding the right doctor and getting to her/his office or learning what is in the newspaper. Old gays may need the help of young gays who can locate the gay-oriented physician and read aloud from the gay newspaper. There are some special problems for older gays who are not able to care for themselves adequately, and we younger gays are becoming more aware daily that we need to help our elders so that we may learn more from them about our own identity and our future.

But the fact remains that gay people have had to learn to

[1] This was a preview of a research reported under the title "Adult Development and Aging: A Gay Perspective," published in a special issue of *The Journal of Social Issues*, Volume 34, 1978. "Psychology and the Gay Community," edited by Dorothy J. Riddle and Stephen F. Morin.

be whole people who could care for themselves and not be limited by silly "sex roles" and that particular type of learning helps one to glide more gracefully into old age. Perhaps our society could learn from this and speed up the effort to get people out of restrictive male, female, mother, father, husband or wife roles.

The old at heart know a wonderful secret about how their body looks and how they wish to present it to the world. Lately there has been a flood of books telling men how to look beautiful. That sort of book has been around for women for decades. The books generally suggest ways to trick people into thinking you are younger (hence more desirable) than you really are. But the old at heart know it is best to present themselves as they really are. They may use some cosmetics, but the desired result is not to look younger but to look your best. Hair the color of dishwater may be enhanced by lightening or darkening. Beautiful eyes that need assistance with vision may be given contact lenses rather than thick spectacles. The effort is made to look your best. It is a gift to others and yourself. But never do the old at heart try to look years younger. I would be an insult to the self.

There continues to be a shortage of intergenerational people in the gay community, and more so in the larger community. We must do what we can to question the taboos and make it safer to reach across this line because it is a silly division that cheats all of us. We are especially in need of youngsters who touch caringly and with wonder and oldsters who return the touch and counsel caringly. If our society can learn the lesson of gays who have dared to cross the age barriers it could save us from the present tyranny of youth and from the impending catastrophe, as the population grows older, of tyranny of the old.

Perhaps most of us can learn to be young in spirit and old at heart whatever our chronological age. What a wonderful world that would be!

16

Early Departures

Death is a natural event in the chain of life. One person moves on and others, influenced by contact with that person, pick up bits and pieces of the life left in memory, shaping and using these bits and pieces in the ongoing development of their own lives.

It is easier to comprehend and accept death when it comes to someone in their eighth or tenth decade of life. But some people are early departures. Illness, accident, and suicide happen. Suddenly the person is gone, leaving only memories where we were anticipating more life. Early departures have a special impact for gay people. We seem to have more of them than is our share. We have had to learn acceptance and understanding. Perhaps a closer look at early departures from life can help all of us, gay and non-gay, to face the phenomenon more honestly and to learn.

A man in his early thirties, whom I shall call George, appeared in my office some years ago saying that he wanted some counseling and had been referred by friends who had worked with me. He had a tall, athletic build and a plain, almost handsome face. His voice was deep and his smile easy. Within minutes it was clear that he was bright and well-educated, with an occupation that permitted him to live comfortably with his lover of ten years who was established in an equally satisfying profession. Only one thing seemed out of keeping with the picture of a happy, successful young man— he walked with the aid of a cane. I asked what he hoped to accomplish with the aid of psychotherapy or counseling and his answer was clear.

A year earlier he learned that he had a degenerative disease. He did not know how many years of life he had ahead but it was unlikely that he would live more than a half dozen years. His disease ran a natural course which included periods of remission during which he and those who loved him were tempted to believe the disease had been arrested. But after each remission of symptoms, the disease would take a heartbreaking plunge forward again. He was not here to find hope, he told me, but to face the reality of his situation and get some help in learning how best to deal with it.

He was straightforward and matter-of-fact in outlining the areas he thought he needed to investigate. What bothered me first was that he was too matter-of-fact, the sorrow and fear were not permitted to show. He said that he had to face his declining sexual attractiveness and understand what that meant to him as a gay man. He also had to face the increasing burden that his degenerative disease created for his lover. He needed to come to terms with his declining ability to define his worth through his work, since his ability to work decreased as the disease continued its course. He had to find ways of compensating for his decreasing physical mobility. He was also unsure now when friends really wanted to be with him and when they were offering pity.

The discovery of a degenerative terminal illness is always a dreadful shock. It was clear that he had handled it as best he could up to now and wanted and needed help in arranging his remaining years. In our individual work together, he found the necessity of opening up honest, if painful, discussions with his lover and using the excellent resources they both had to solve each new problem the disease presented. They had to learn, for instance, a constant rearrangement of their sex life so that the needs of each of them would best be met. He learned to tell friends when he was not sure if they were acting out of pity and ask them please not to do so because he needed his pride. He discovered the strain had produced some feelings he was reluctant to admit to himself, such as feeling sorry for himself and angry at his fate; he was aware that moments of dark despair were too heavy for him to shoulder alone. They were also sometimes overwhelming for his lover and close friends when he confided in them. Some of these feelings were too frightening and worrisome for the people who were closest to him.

He was reluctant to enter an ongoing group of gay men because he felt he would be entering as a second-class citizen and that people would shy away from him. But he took the risk and learned there were other people in the gay community willing to help him to shoulder his burden. They helped him to see that he brought them a gift by letting them face their own mortality and their responsibility to others, and by permitting them to draw on his example of strength while offering what help they could. During the last year of his life, before he was too weak to leave the house, he was carried into the group each week by members who seated him on a throne of cushions, making jokes about queens while offering uncomplicated love. He taught us a lot and we helped him. He helped everyone to learn how necessary it is to ask for help when it is needed, how to find acceptance and even some relief as death draws nearer, and how to protect the amount of privacy needed to meet one's own end. When he died, we sat in a circle holding hands, eyes closed, silently remembering him together. It felt as if he was there with us for that farewell. We had our tears, but we were glad for him too.

And there is the woman who lived for many years with her lover. They pretended to the world that they were not gay— just two women living together. Fortunately, they had a few close gay friends. Her lover developed a terminal illness that kept her bedridden for several years. The woman I know nursed her to the end, abandoning her job and using up the money they had saved together. She found herself alone in her sixties, supported emotionally and financially by those gay friends, having to face developing a livelihood for herself once more, and having to face the search for another mate because she learned that living alone was unbearable for her.

And the man who came to my office distraught, sent by his physician because of severe high blood pressure. He had not been able to tell his physician that his "roommate" who had died of a sudden and unexpected heart attack six months earlier was his lover of twenty years. He was bereft and in agony with his mourning, absolutely alone because they had kept their relationship a secret and thought they needed only one another. He had not permitted himself to cry at the funeral for fear of what people would think. He had to learn to find friends and to tell his story again and again, like a bad dream, until the tears had done their work, the mourning could proceed with support.

It seems unreal to prepare oneself for the possibility of a terminal illness or to face the possibility that a lover or friend may suddenly succumb to such an illness. Yet it is a fact of life. Gay people have been patching one another up for decades in the aftermath of such an event, not feeling able to draw on the usual support of the community at large. We have learned to cover some of our fear of such an event with dark humor, but increasingly, as we bring our lifestyle into the light of day, we see that we have the right and the obligation to face this fact of life openly. Lovers and friends must talk through the possibilities and hear one another's wishes.

Accidents happen. They come out of the blue and one can never be prepared. Again it is necessary to consider the possibility that sudden accidental death, disfigurement, or disability may occur to oneself, a lover, or a friend. Feelings and plans must be talked out. Gay people know the necessity of this because our society's institutions too often fail us and we must carry the burden ourselves. In the planning and sorting of feelings no promises can be made. That works in movies, but in real life people change constantly. But talking it out permits more consciousness and more preparedness. I had a client in psychotherapy for a year whose best friend had been murdered in another state. The friend had unwisely taken home a drunken man who turned out to be filled with self-loathing and believed it his duty to kill as many queers as possible. My client said, "He was there all the time, only a phone call away—always ready for life and full of new ideas, always ready to help. And then one day a phone call comes with another voice at the other end and my best friend does not exist any more! He was only twenty-seven and he never hurt anyone!" He, too, had to cry the tears that would begin to ease the shock and learn to reach out to others for support.

And I recall a man who died in a motorcycle accident. Desperately in love with a man who teased him with his unavailability, he was not willing to face his own frustration and anger. It would have meant starting to let go of the romantic dream of true love. I wonder if that stored-up anger and frustration did not contribute to the accident. His desired man was with him but received only a few bruises. Some honest admission of feelings might have saved that life.

A woman's lover was killed in a commercial plane crash and she learned about it days later from her lover's sister. Almost no one had suspected they were lovers. She had to learn to admit their lover relationship after the death. It was a bad dream. She had to talk about the reality. She had to release her anger. In order to do that she had to disclose herself as a gay woman. Then her anger and sorrow were followed by a flow of other feelings that had been locked up inside, creating a massive depression along with heavy dependence on alcohol that had caused her to lose her job.

And I could tell of the stunningly beautiful young man who

thought he had lost his life in an accident because he lost an arm and a leg. He has to struggle to gain a new understanding of himself and his assets. He thought his life was over because he could not longer stroll into a bar and take home almost any man he desired. First he learned that he still had his good looks, his winning smile, and his wit. Slowly he learned that he was not a second-class citizen because he was missing two limbs. This learning came more slowly because a lot of society views disabled people as second-class and he had not yet come to terms with his feeling inferior because he was gay. One positive result of the accident is that the family who had turned him out into the streets learned that they were happy to have a gay son who is still alive. And he is learning that his superficial beauty would have faded anyway. He has learned to develop more lasting assets while still young.

There was a woman with too many scars from too many operations who made herself impressively fat to keep away the hurtful possibility of love with another woman, since she did not see how that love could ever be returned. She was very nearly an early departure who ate herself to death. She has learned to redefine herself. She was never a beauty, as she now admits, and always feared unrequited love from other women. The scars and the operations seemed like proof positive of what she had always known. She is no longer hiding her fear and bitterness, so it is slowly draining away. It is being replaced by a smile that shows self-acceptance and knowledge of the possibility of love. She has learned to be thankful for her natural assets, including a good mind and a great sense of rhythm. She has learned to trust admiration and to trust small feelings of love sometimes. She says, "Who knows, maybe I'll marry a geriatric go-go dancer some day!"

We have all known people who have a premonition that they are destined to die young. When they talk about it, I often sense a touch of glamour and suspect they have seen too many old movies. Often it is an excuse for not taking charge of one's life, since "It will be over all too soon, anyway." Such a person may or may not be an early departure, but he or she can be shown the folly of a "do-nothing" orientation to life. A kick in the pants is needed, along with a strong suggestion that, since it is to be a short lifetime, the person had better hurry and decide how it is to be used so as to be proud of it when it ends. The truth is that many of these romantic would-be early departures who want to leave with a good-looking corpse live to be quite old, once they discover there is more to life than the care and pleasuring of the body. It is a lack of feelings of self-worth showing through, as well as fear. Friends are more helpful when they recognize the fright, point out assets that are there, and offer support while the person works to develop additional assets. Romantic early condolences do not help.

Suicide is a difficult and complex phenomenon to deal with in a culture that is phobic about death. Some individuals seem drawn to death through many years of their life or throughout their whole lifetime. It is part of the phenomenon we do not understand. With such people it seems almost a part of their makeup and, no matter how hard they try to stay alive or how much others try to help them stay alive, it ends in suicide.

Gay people are more familiar with suicide and suicide attempts than the rest of society. Our subculture is treated punitively by the larger society and lacks the usual support of a biological family that is in the same subculture. Too often the new family cannot be built fast enough, the pressures mount, there is more ugly harassment than a person feels able to handle, and suicide is seen as the only way out of the suffering that seems unendurable. When a suicide succeeds under these circumstances, I wonder how the pious hatemongers of our world can live with themselves.

There are other circumstances in suicides. I knew one man whose entire life was geared for struggle. He came out quite publicly as a gay person and worked hard to help other gays.

He was a fighter and a helper, but he could never find the love and other satisfactions he wanted in his own life. And then a "right man" appeared. Love entered his life and some of the other pieces of his life puzzle that had been missing began to fall into place. He seemed happy but dazed, bewildered by his good fortune. There was some hint that he did not know how to live this new life wherein the amount of struggle was minimal. He had made suicide attempts at earlier periods in his life and failed. This time he made one and succeeded. There was some suggestion that his love affair was on the wane. It is hard to know if he found the prospect of the old life unbearable after a taste of honey, or if he questioned his ability to be happy with that which he had sought all his life. But he left a note saying that he was tired and took his secret with him when he took his life.

There is the woman who hanged herself because she could not find a way to say "yes" to her gay identity. She could not get the world, as represented by her family, to agree that it was possible to be a decent, respectable person and be gay. She could find no way to not be gay and there seemed no other way out. She needed to feel that she was in harmony or accord with the world and could not stay alive long enough without it to build her own self-validation. Until we have a society that publicly supports the viability of alternate lifestyles, there will be some people, like this woman, who will be lost because they realize they do not fit the mold they think they should, and they are too honest to lie.

And I knew a man who killed himself with pills and alcohol because his attempts to kill the pain of isolation and self-loathing with alcohol and indiscriminate sexual activity made him feel even less worthwhile. He was caught in a downward spiral. If we had had a gay-oriented mental health center with a live-in facility staffed by understanding gay professionals, a stay of a month there, protected from the assaults of a homophobic world, might have saved his life. He was a talented person, and if he had survived he would have paid back the debt one hundred fold in the next two decades of his life. So far, our society does not care enough to save such a man.

There was the gay woman who shot herself. She felt trapped in a job where she believed that everyone whispered about her, suspecting that she had homosexual feelings. I am sure they did whisper about her because she was odd. Their merry harassment had made her odd. Her knowledge of her inner secret made her vulnerable. She said that she was so lonely at night. She was an attractive, good-hearted woman, who could have been a wonderful lifetime companion for another woman. But she feared opening herself to the love of another woman because the whole world would know about her homosexuality then and everyone would point and laugh. What a waste. She did no one any harm and hid only her capacity to love.

And finally, let me tell of the teenage girl who walked briskly, smiling, onto the bridge and, halfway across, leaped over the rail to meet her death in the water below. No one knew why. Her boyfriend found the answer when the high school principal let him clean out her locker. Scribbled notes in the guise of a story, hidden in the rear flap of her binder told her story. She was gay and she knew it, but her mother had been active in crusading against gay rights. She knew nothing positive about gay people, believed she had been cursed, and dared not disgrace the family. And so she killed herself. Her boyfriend, ironically, was gay also and had not yet found the courage to tell her. They could have made it through together but they were both too scared to trust one another. The experience turned him into an overnight gay radical, but he curbed his impulse to confront the mother with the reason for the girl's suicide. He felt guilty about it himself and felt he owed his girlfriend the right to her decision about her death even if that decision was made in a cloud of confusion and misunderstanding created with the active help of her mother. That mother mourns her daughter in mystery still, not knowing that she helped to kill her.

We do not know enough about some of these suicides to know how to prevent them. Those who could have been saved will be followed by others like them until our society finds enough sanity to value differences and is willing to pay for mental health facilities aimed at offering special help to special subgroups. When a gay person is institutionalized almost anywhere in America, he or she is only headed for more trouble. As a society, we have the know-how but not the willingness to stop some of these early departures. Until a day of enlightenment, we gay people must continue to help each other as best we can, building support systems and harnessing our anger at a society that is wrong.

If you or someone you know sees suicide as a real option when things are not going well, it is a good idea to have an emergency plan that can be activated without too much trouble. Someone wrote me in a letter, "I have told others and myself things I could do when I'm really in depression—like writing for myself, *before* the depression comes, a list of things I would like to do and have not yet done, places I love that are peaceful, trips I would like to take, and even possible job opportunities or ways of making a living other than what I'm doing that could be explored profitably. I have also made agreements with people in my support system that when the blue meanies strike, the other person or I will make at least one phone call a day, stay on for at least five minutes, and tell the truth."

I have suggested to people in ongoing groups that they depend on one another rather than on one person such as a therapist. The group can keep an up-to-date list of members with addresses and phone numbers. People can save old lists, including information on those who have left the group but are still important in their lives. When in trouble, they can go down the list and call every person until they reach enough people to feel the pressure has eased. Sometimes it helps to go spend the night at someone's house, both for the emotional nourishment and the change of scene. I think everyone should have such a list. It is as important as keeping the telephone numbers of police, fire station, and ambulance nearby.

Time brings change, but in a desperate moment you must have reachable sources of help. If you do not have those sources of help today, it is an urgent priority to develop them starting now.

How to say goodbye to someone who is an early departure? When the death is inevitable as in terminal illness, the goodbyes must be said. Truth is more kind than denial. To pretend that someone is not dying when they sense that they are makes the burden heavier by adding unreality. Much is now being written about dying. Loved ones can help the dying person to take charge of his or her death. Touching someone who is dying, touching them physically, is important. They can feel your love and all of the feelings that are too hard to put into words. And when you touch, you truly touch your own mortality, the chain of life that leads to an end. Somehow that sort of touching makes it all more natural. A parting of loved ones deserves a goodbye.

Suicides and accidental deaths are almost always a surprise. We all need to practice saying goodbye and keeping our emotional communication up to date with the people whom we love.

At the end of weekend groups, we sit in a circle and focus on one member of the group at a time. Each other person in the group thinks how he would feel if he were never to see this person again. What, if anything, has been left unsaid. It is a last chance before the artificial community of the weekend ends to bring the relationship up-to-date and say whatever has not been said. Some of the people described in this chapter have participated in a weekend group. Other members of the group unknowingly were saying a very real goodbye. When it has happened that someone from the group has died before another person from the group saw him again, it has always been a source of comfort that they were up-to-date on their last meeting. The goodbye is sometimes as simple as "I want you to know that what I most value about you is your dedication to making this a better world." Or, "I want you to know that I appreciate the beauty of your smile, the way you move, and your willingness to share that beauty as unself-consciously as a garden full of summer flowers." Or "I like your flash of contagious enthusiasm." Or, "Your tears are beautiful and I'll never forget them." Or sometimes a rock-bottom honest statement like, "I want you to know that I like and respect you and hope you stay alive, but if you have to go, I'll try to understand. Sometimes somebody has to leave a party early, before people have really had a chance to get to know him. Nobody wants him to go but he has to go. You miss him but you understand."

There is the matter of mourning. Mourning is a natural process. It is harder when you mourn an early departure. There is more to try to understand than when a person dies of natural causes in old age. Mourning work is hard work. It leaves you feeling tired for weeks or months.

Much of the work is done by your unconscious while you are asleep or while you are daydreaming. Do not be surprised if you find yourself distracted or tired during a period of mourning. Sometimes you need to talk to the person who has died, inside your own mind. There are things that have been left unsaid. Or there are things that have been said that need saying again, like "I miss you." Sometimes you need the reassurance that you can reach across the void and call the person to you in your mind's eye and reminisce about the past or think about the future. All of this can help you to bear the pain. And do not be surprised if you find some irrational anger. Inside we are all still children and the small child does not understand why someone would die and go away "if they really loved me."

Memories and other symptoms of mourning will come up less and less frequently over time and they generally become less and less vivid. But once someone has been alive for you in your life and emotions, they will never be gone completely, and you can expect memories of them for the rest of your life. It is the part of them that stays alive: the memories they have left in you and other people whom they touched during their lifetime.

Gay Pride Day falls on the Sunday in June closest to the anniversary of the 1969 Stonewall riots in New York City. There are parades, celebrations and speeches, and it offers us a chance to gather together and feel our wholeness and diversity as a gay community. I also make use of Gay Pride Day as a day of mourning or a Day of the Dead. It is a time I remember the gay people who are no longer alive, particularly the early departures. Remembering them keeps them alive for me, and it keeps me alive as a gay person.

17

Final Curtain

We are born alone and we die alone. That is a simple fact of nature that has been explored by many philosophers. Today is my daughter's birthday, and I am remembering the moment of her birth. She was attended during the birth process by a loving mother, a loving father, and a genuinely caring medical staff. We all cried with joy when she entered our world. But that first moment of her birth, she was subjectively alone in the world, as she will be in her last moment of life, though she may be surrounded then by the family she has created and acquired. We are in the habit of thinking that it is the biological family that sees us into and out of this world but the truth is that our attendants at the end are acquired family. No one is more conscious of this than the gay person. Most gay people face the painful truth during their lifetime that their biological family does not understand them. We have to accept that, usually, and reach out into the world to find others who *will* understand and love us for the person each of us truly is.

We gay people have a responsibility to ourselves and to one

another. We must learn the ways to help one another live and, when the time comes, to help one another die. This book has been full of our struggle to free ourselves from prescriptions for living that do not fit us. Our struggle is to free ourselves from people who believe they care for us while acting as agents of a culture opposed to us, thereby inadvertently persecuting us when we are most defenseless. Looking at our ways of living, loving, aging, and dying, it becomes increasingly clear that we must learn to go out in the world and find our own kind, the people who appreciate us. More often than not these are other gay people. They understand more readily because they have walked a similar path. Some non-gay people, because of their own unusual life experiences in a world that rarely appreciates the unusual, are able to reach across the line of segregation, match understanding with caring, and become loved ones.

I hope that I have exploded the myth that to be old and gay means being lonely and miserable. We seem to do a better-than-average job of seeing to it that our last years are satisfying. But we could make them better. During the last decade, while we have been struggling for public recognition of our right to exist in this society, we have given a lot of attention to the earlier years of our lives. We have tried to communicate the loneliness and unreality that exists for us then. We still have not begun to face honestly the painful plight of the children who have an awareness of their gay identity and must remain silent prisoners until they have served their time and become legal adults. But we have helped some of the world to understand what our early adult years are like. We can harness the enormous talent and strength accumulated during the mature years in the gay community and use these resources to provide a dazzling monument to our achievements as a group.

A year ago I was asked to be on a board of advisors for a community to be built in Southern California for aging gays. My reply was an eager "yes." My fantasies of the possibilities probably do not match those of other people who would be on the board, but that just means more opportunity to take divergent views and build something better than any *one* of us could conceive alone.

Imagine a town created by and for gay people, where our difference is appreciated and age is seen as an asset. Not a nursing home sort of place, but a place where our collective experience and talents could construct a positive society that could reach into the world by example and teach the worth of age and diversity of lifestyle. We certainly have the talent.

My hope is that it would start as a small village or town and grow. A place for gay people in their final quadrant of life. Older gays would have the collective wisdom to know that we are not building a utopia because we have learned that nothing is perfect. We know how to compromise and make do while building something better. My vision is of a place where we can help one another learn to live and learn to die, where uniformity is not a value. And younger gays would be encouraged to come as guests, to help, knowing that they are building something for their own future.

Imagine buildings created by the best talent of gay architects, designers, contractors, and construction workers using the wisdom of gay community planners. We could draw on the resources of gay statesmen, artists, peacekeepers, athletes. It would begin as a home town for those aging gays who cannot or do not wish to finish their years in total independence. I hope it would be in a location where the weather is kind and the scenery nourishing—at the seaside, near a lake, or in the mountains with plenty of fresh air and quiet. Our pool of talent should be able to provide plenty of activities to individuals who are interested. We could have a topnotch medical and counseling staff. It could be a community in which skin hunger need not exist, where touching is easy. There could be parties for those who enjoy them and orgies for those who still find vigorous sexuality amusing. It could be a town where there is something for everyone, with minimal rules that protect the right to privacy and the tranquility for rest and reflection. The younger gays who would come to visit and learn could volunteer youthful muscle and ideas and participate in the touching, talking, artistry, and learning. Imagine a symphony orchestra, opera company, and even a corps de ballet (where the challenge of the choreographers would be to use the artistic instruments of aging bodies in the most aesthetically pleasing possible manner). We could have amateur groups too, certainly, but our major symphony, opera, theatre, and ballet companies would be highly professional artistic demonstration projects that would capture the imagination of the world.

I envision a community that is constantly growing, organic, because its roots are in fertile soil. Imagine the gay university that could develop in such a community—a place where questions are honored more than answers. And, more than any other goal, this community could be devoted to searching for optimal use of the final years of life, and to making death a truly individual final statement. There would be arms to comfort and support those near death when fright and uncertainty are experienced. No one would need to be alone except when they desired aloneness for meditation and contemplation. And of course, the food would be superb! I think our biggest problem would be to keep the rest of the world out, or to welcome them in limited numbers. The danger would be that we might become a tourist mecca.

I hope that we do build such a community. If I am ablebodied up to the end I would probably not want to live there all of the time, but imagine that I would want to keep a home there while continuing to explore the rest of the world. But what a wonderful, proud home it would be to have waiting for me!

Which brings us to a major question all lively aging people think about in the final years of life: What do I still want to do before I go? What are the challenges? What is the unfinished business? Knowing that the clock and physical limitations will not permit me to do everything, what are the things

I most want to do? If I have not done so before I reach those
final years, I believe I would want to live for extended periods of time in several different countries where I could learn
the language, the mind set, customs, and the flora and fauna.
I know it would broaden me and broaden the ways in which I
am able to conceptualize and search out questions about
human life. It is important to me in the final years of life that
I broaden my scope rather than restrict it. I may need more
time to rest my body but my mind can be busy.

I would also like to have plenty of time for writing as well
as contemplation in my final years. Writing has always been
my best means of finding and assembling my thoughts and
feelings. Again, I would hope that it would broaden my
scope. And I want to have time to sit in the sun, look at the
ocean, be confronted with works of art, read books, and listen to nature—it has so much to teach. All of that will give
me the stimulus to sort my memories and continue to try to
better my understanding of what my life has been about.

And what would *you* want? People are unfinished in so
many different ways. Do you need to show off? Do penance?
Climb a mountain? The end is so like the beginning. In the
beginning years of my life there was so much need to understand, but I did not know how to go about it. I wondered why
people were not kind to one another so that everyone could
feel a little better no matter how harsh the circumstances or
physical surroundings. And now when I project ahead to my
final years, I see that I am trying to broaden my scope, gain
more tools that will help in that quest for understanding.

As I look for examples in the lives of others, it makes me
chuckle to think of one person I know who spent the early
years of his life in active pursuit of sex and will probably
spend his final years the same way. He once told me that he
remembered making a solemn vow to himself as a tiny child
to give up sex until he got to kindergarten! And I think of a
friend who spent the early years of her life actively searching
for the right place to settle herself, like a dog or a cat moving

in circles trying to find just the right spot to lie down. I imagine her final years will be spent trying to find the right spot(s) to settle.

This phenomenon of the end being similar to the beginning is not so much the completion of a circle as a return to a related spot on a spiral. My search for understanding is not nearly as survival-oriented now. It is more global, peaceful, and philosophical. My friend's sexual search is much less driven by need and much more motivated by enjoyment of the beauty and mystery of that particular facet of life. And the place search is now much less a matter of trying to be right, and much more an appreciative reflection of the cosmic joke that there is no "right" place. We three are all in our middle years of life, so it will be interesting to see how the end is like the beginning but different—if it is a spiral and not a circle.

I sometimes wonder whether operas imitate life or vice versa. There certainly is a direct connection that keeps audiences dedicated to opera generation after generation. Death is terribly important in so many operas. We make fun of the improbable final aria sung by a dying person. But those final arias are important. They sum up the essence of the character and provide a final statement. The members of the audience are able to take the final statement and apply it in their own lives in the hours, months, and years that follow the performance.

Death is, or can be, that final aria for each of us—the statement that makes the lifetime whole. Communicated to those who are to go on living, we have offered something that can be used by them in building and arranging their own lives. At that moment of death, when you are alone as you were at your moment of birth, there must be an awareness that there is to be no more personal life. Your life has been lived and the remembered aspects of it will become the property of other living people now, just as your body slowly returns to its sources and becomes the property of the universe in which it

began. No matter what one's religious beliefs or lack of religious beliefs, this is the simple fact of life.

What is your final aria, your final personal statement if
this were to be the last day of your life? For many of us that is
too hard a question to answer. We live in a culture phobic
about death and devote considerable energy to avoiding this
question. But it is worth thinking about. Living with your
death can clarify the path of your life and increase the quality of satisfaction with living. As life keeps changing, so does
your final statement. Why not take some time to think about
what message you need to leave for those who will live after
you, and the form in which you choose to leave it. An artist
leaves his or her work. Parents leave children. All of us leave
memories in the minds of others. But is that enough? Is there
something more you would like to say if you knew this were
your last day?

For most of us, a periodic review of what our life has been
about would provide a useful focus. It might be good to do it
annually, like a yearly physical checkup. It would offer an
opportunity for an up-to-date final aria in case the last moment catches us by surprise. I keep a journal and I like to take
a look at my life each year on my birthday, recording my
thoughts and feelings in my journal, but that is more like
notes to myself. A note to those who are to go on living would
be based on more reflection and offer a better summing up.
Our traditions permit suicide notes and wills that dictate the
disposition of material property, but a final summation
would require a new tradition. Your summary statement
might not be great literature and might never make it to the
Library of Congress, but it would mean a lot to those who
care about you and have watched you live. I should think it
would provide most people with a greater feeling of peace
and acceptance when the last moment comes.

I tried making such a statement for myself while making
notes for this final chapter of this book. I found that it was all
too easy to turn it into a huge chore. I began by trying to

leave a few personal words to each person who is important in my life and found it was becoming as meaningless as the task of getting Christmas cards out all in one great rush or sending postcards from a vacation spot rather than enjoying the vacation. After some thought, I realized that what worked better for me was a short summary statement having to do with my present satisfactions with life as it has been up to now, with just a few direct notes to the people who are most important in my life. It is less a chore and makes a satisfying final aria. I found that it must be done in the frame of mind that assumes one's life will continue but is similar to the farewells discussed in the last chapter—"Were I never to see you again, I would want you to know . . ."

And there is another task to be taken care of before the end. Death comes unexpectedly sometimes but it does come to each of us sooner or later. Part of our adult responsibility is taking charge of the event of our death in much the same way we have learned to take charge of the course of our adult lives. There are questions to be answered. What sort of ceremony, if any, do you think would be appropriate for the end of your life? Does it matter to you? It may be that once life is finished, you would prefer to leave the choice of disposition and ceremony to a particular person or persons—to do that which will help them the most. Whatever the choice, it would be good to communicate your thoughts about it while still living. What if there is to be a debilitating illness before death? Who is to care for you and how are finances to be handled? Who is to make the decisions? Will your affairs be in order? If not, who is to tidy up after you and are they willing to do so? It keeps changing along with life, and your will and final statement must keep pace with that change so that it is up to date. Our death-phobic orientation may make these thoughts seem morbid, but they are quite practical.

For gay people and many others in our society, the old rules of next-of-kin do not fit and may represent disaster. Too many gay people have not provided for their death in ways that are legally binding. If you do not wish it all simply dumped into the lap of your nearest kin, you had better see a gay-oriented lawyer quickly. Lovers have been left not only bereft, but destitute, while homophobic legal relatives who have had little to do with a person's life take over at death.

As you contemplate the finish of your lifetime and review what has been, you may find yourself asking, "Is that all there is?" The answer is "Yes." What your life has been, the memories you leave behind, the final satisfactions and dissatisfactions, are all there is. And if that is not enough it is your own responsibility. A life that has not been satisfying usually reveals a life that has been lived by following tracks put down for you by others. The key to a satisfying life that can be ended in pride and dignity, as gay people have learned, is the will to forge your own trail, make your own mistakes, learn from them, find your own surprises, joys and sorrows, and cope with your own misfortunes. That is all there is, but it can be more than enough because it is your own life, lived the best way you knew how, and it has yielded the greatest possible satisfaction. No life is perfect, but many are good.

And when the final curtain is down, we are off to the next adventure that has produced so much speculation, ritual, and unnecessary fear. Death can be accepted as birth was— uncharted territory that is simply the next step. It is the end of the personal lifetime. Identity remains only in the memories of others who will shape it according to their own needs.

In the forever of eternity we are all gay finally—freed at last from the confines of petty dictates of taste, conduct, and categorization. We freely recombine with all of nature, so rich and vast in its diversity that there is no *hetero* or *homo*. All is a natural combining and separating that is cosmically sexual.

Living, loving, aging, and dying. From a gay perspective, our world has made it so much more complicated than was necessary. Perhaps one day each of us will be free to follow our destiny without condemnation. Struggle can make a person strong, but we have lost too many along the way.

Books of Related Interest

LOVING SOMEONE GAY by Don Clark, Ph.D., offers sensitive, intelligent guidance to gays and those who care about them from a gay therapist who has specialized in clinical psychology for the past nine years. 192 pages, hardcover, $9.95

POSITIVELY GAY, edited by Betty Berzon, Ph.D., and Robert Leighton, offers gay people creative new options for achieving a positive gay image that integrates personal, political and economic concerns. 192 pages, soft cover, $4.95

I DESERVE LOVE by Sondra Ray presents specific exercises in a variety of areas, including sex, love, self-esteem, affection and trust, to name a few. You have the power to achieve whatever goals you pursue. 128 pages, soft cover, $3.95

HOW TO BE SOMEBODY by Yetta Bernhard offers a specific guide for personal growth that will lead to acceptance to one's self as a human being. Bernhard is a noted psychologist who offers advice that can change your life. 96 pages, soft cover, $3.95

In **SELF-CARE**, Yetta Bernhard tells her reader to say "I count " and describes exactly how to put the premise of self-care into practical, everyday living. 252 pages, soft cover, $6.95

WHERE WILL I BE TOMORROW? by Walter Rinder shows exceptional sensitivity, speaking in prose, poetry, and eloquent photography of the love of a man for another man. 144 pages, soft cover, $4.95

Available at your local book or department store or directly from the publisher. To order by mail, send check or money order to:

Celestial Arts
231 Adrian Road
Millbrae, CA 94030

Please include $1.00 for postage and handling. California residents add 6% tax.